Praise for

UNWRITTEI

T0267507

"*Unwritten* is the book every first-time author of a
the book anyone contemplating whether to becon~~.... ......~~
you through all the key components of writing and publishing a book, from start to
finish. A quick read packed with valuable action items, you'll walk away knowing your
next steps, no matter where you are on your journey. If you feel lost or overwhelmed
at the thought of taking your great big idea from manuscript draft to published book,
this book is for you."

— **HEIDI SCOTT GIUSTO, PHD,** #1 bestselling author of *The 3rd Paradigm* and owner
of Career Path Writing Solutions

"Emily Crookston's *Unwritten* makes writing a business book unscary. I'm working
on my fourth business book, and this 'savvy best friend' can guide you through the
weird, wild world of self-publishing. Her writing style is like a casual coffee shop
chat—approachable, relatable, and honest. She's not here to paint rainbows and
unicorns but to lay out the real deal about the hustle and hard work to be published.
Fear not, though; she's armed you with the roadmap in this book to write it in a way
that is sustainable and doesn't consume your life."

— **MARCEY RADER,** productivity speaker, coach, three-time author, and founder of
RaderCo

"Emily's passion for writing and commitment to excellence have left an indelible mark
on me. I've had the privilege of witnessing her dedication and unique approach to
writing firsthand.
     Her approach to writing is nothing short of inspiring. She weaves words with
finesse, transforming complex ideas into accessible narratives. Emily's ability to distill
intricate concepts into actionable insights is something I have truly valued.
     Unwritten is a treasure trove of wisdom—a roadmap for entrepreneurs, leaders,
and dreamers alike. Emily's words will ignite motivation, spark innovation, and provide
readers with new perspectives. Emily's impact is bound to resonate far beyond the
pages of her book, and I'm grateful she's sharing her gifts and talents with the world."

— **WILLIAM WASHINGTON,** chief financial officer, Baker McKenzie

"*Unwritten* turns the daunting and overwhelming task of writing a book into something
that feels doable (and even easy) from the very first chapter. Emily expertly guides you
to create a book that you not only finish and publish but also creates demand for your
work. If you are a business owner who wants to write a book that results in sales for
your offer, get this book now!"

— **MICHELLE MAZUR, PHD,** author of *3 Word Rebellion* and host of *Make
Marketing Suck Less*

www.amplifypublishinggroup.com

*Unwritten: The Thought Leader's Guide to Not Overthinking
Your Business Book*

For more information, please contact:
Amplify Publishing, an imprint of Amplify Publishing Group
620 Herndon Parkway, Suite 220
Herndon, VA 20170
info@amplifypublishing.com

Library of Congress Control Number: 2023923524

CPSIA Code: PRV0624A

ISBN-13: 979-8-89138-204-6

Printed in the United States

For the part of you (and me) that overthinks the writing and underthinks everything else.

UN

The Thought Leader's Guide to

WRIT

Not Overthinking Your Business Book

TEN

EMILY CROOKSTON

amplify
an imprint of Amplify Publishing Group

CONTENTS

INTRODUCTION

Welcome! You're here because you're a business owner, and you want to write a business book. That's why you picked up my book, and I'm so excited you did.

You might also see yourself as a thought leader or an aspiring thought leader. Personally, my relationship with this buzzword is fraught,* but here's my simple definition:

A thought leader is an expert who owns their expertise.

While you might think of yourself as a thought leader, if you want others to think of you in that way, then you need a platform, and you

---

* I'm always skeptical of people who call themselves "thought leaders." This feels like a title that should be earned. Also, the image I have of a thought leader is a Gary Vee type running around on stage, wearing a headset in front of a giant moving picture of himself projected on the screen. I don't see my clients in this image. I want all big idea experts to have a seat at the table.

need to cultivate what I call your thought leadership ecosystem. This is what it means to own your expertise. And your book is one piece of your thought leadership ecosystem, which is why it's so important not to overthink the book and underthink all of the other pieces (more on this later).

Above all of this, though, you're something more. At your very core, you're an "idea" person. You're a subject matter expert, but you're not merely someone who has put in the 10,000 hours.* You have a unique perspective on your industry or your work that you are ready to share with the world. In other words, you have big ideas. You're what I call a big idea expert.

And you want to write a book because you have a big idea that won't leave you. Perhaps you've tried to shake it off, but it just won't let you go. After all, writing a book isn't very convenient when you own and run a business. Most business owners who write their own books write on the weekend, early in the morning, or late at night after they put the kids to bed and their partner is passed out on the couch. We write in the cracks and crevices of our businesses and our lives. You're making a sacrifice by embarking on this journey to write your own book, but you're doing it because you can't let that big idea marinate any longer. You're ready to set it free. You're ready to get it out of your head and into the hands of your fans, clients, and prospects.

YOU AND YOUR BIG IDEA: A SYMBIOTIC RELATIONSHIP

I see the sacrifice you're making to chase down this big idea. You're not doing it from a place of ego—you're not some god ready to impose your will on the words. The idea is in the driver's seat, and you're the

---

* Malcolm Gladwell introduces what he calls the "10,000-hour rule" in his book *Outliers: The Story of Success*, asserting that the key to achieving success is to practice in the correct way for 10,000 hours.

copilot. This is not to downplay your role as the author, though. By writing your book, you are entering into a symbiotic relationship with your big idea. It's mutually beneficial. You gain authority, credibility, and recognition as a big idea expert, while your big idea gets to exist in the world. What a beautiful thing!

Despite this sacrifice, you're no martyr. You wouldn't be here if you didn't believe you need a book for your business and that there is a clear business case for your book. You're not here to *simply* leave a legacy or tell your story (as if either of these things were really simple). This book that you're writing will benefit you and your business. It will allow you to reach a wider audience, gain PR opportunities, speak on bigger stages, increase your consulting fees, etc. And rest assured that this book that I'm writing will teach you how to maximize those benefits.

Having a symbiotic relationship with your book idea means that your big idea needs you as much as you need your big idea. Get comfortable with this relationship, and everything about the process of writing your book gets easier.

"SHOULD I EVEN WRITE THIS BOOK?"

Even though you may feel everything I've said deep down to your core, you may still wonder whether you *should* write this book. Fair warning: this is a question that you will likely ask yourself over and over again right up until your book launch. As much as I'm rooting for you, I also want to leave room for the possibility that writing a book might not be for you (or it might not be for you *now*). And if that's where you find yourself at any moment, I hope you'll give yourself permission not to write your book yourself or not to write your book at all.

No one in their right mind would ever suggest that writing a book while running a business is easy. When I mention that I'm writing this book, people often suggest or imply that it must be easy for me since

I'm a professional ghostwriter. But I don't think that writing is particularly easy for anyone. And while it's true that I find it easier to write for my clients than to write for myself, many days, writing feels like pulling teeth—especially frustrating on days after I've been particularly prolific—and I find myself doing absolutely anything (including rearranging my desk for the 100th time) to avoid the writing that I need to do.

If you find writing to be hard, it's not because you aren't "good" at writing or because you don't have something worthwhile to say. It's because writing is f*cking hard. And this doesn't even take into account what it feels like to try to write *while* running your business full-time. To be honest, the fact that writing is so painful for so many people is the whole reason my business, The Pocket PhD, exists. Every week, my team and I work with thought leaders to identify their big ideas, cultivate their thought leadership ecosystems, build their confidence, and write their books. So whether you choose to write your own book or hire me to ghostwrite it for you, don't assume that since writing is hard, you shouldn't do it.

Okay, what *will* help you answer this question, then? To figure out whether you should write your book, reflect on two things:

1. Whether writing a book is the highest and best use of your time
2. How satisfying you find the process of writing or how satisfying you will find having completed your own book

Writing your book while running your business will be one of the hardest things you'll ever do. This is true, by the way, whether you grew up loving to write, and writing your own content for your business is your favorite part of the week, or you grew up dreading

English class, and you outsource as much of your content writing as possible. Becoming a business book author is hard precisely because there is always something else you could be doing instead, which means that even as you try to focus on your book, you'll feel the pull of a million other things. In these moments, you will have to decide whether writing your book is the highest and best use of your time. And I hope you'll give yourself grace if and when you choose to set your book to the side. Yes, writing your book will be one of the hardest things you'll ever do, but I hope that when the writing happens, it's also one of the most satisfying things you'll ever do, because if writing your book yourself is all pain and no satisfaction, then you shouldn't do it.

If that last sentence stopped you in your tracks, good. That tells me you're paying attention. Let me repeat: if writing your book yourself is all pain and no satisfaction, then you shouldn't do it.

Now, if this feels totally deflating, please take a deep breath before throwing this book across the room (and if you're reading on an electronic device, then maybe find another outlet for your frustration), and let me remind you of two things: (a) just because you shouldn't write your book now doesn't mean you should never write it, and (b) there are other ways to get your book written without writing it yourself. I'm suggesting that you consider the possibility that you shouldn't write your own book not because I'm a ghostwriter, and I want you to call me (though I would certainly take your call), but because I want you to thoroughly examine *why* you want to write this book (more on this in Chapter 2).

To help clarify, if you don't have good answers to the following three "why" questions, then you shouldn't write your book (at least, not now):

1. Why do I want to write this book?
2. Why is now the right time to write this book?

3.   Am I the best person to write this book?

There's no shame in deciding that writing a book is not the best investment you could make in your business right now. Sure, If you have the resources, you could hire a team to help you, but keep in mind also that there are many vehicles for getting that big idea out into the world. For example, you could present your big idea in smaller chunks, like blog or Substack articles or social media posts. You could also share your ideas via video, audio, or in-person workshops. In fact, these are all great ways to test ideas and dip your toes into the pool with other big idea experts. It pays for you to consider where you are in the grand scheme of things and what would help you most—right now—in getting the word out. Considering your content strategy is another way to own your expertise.

All of this is to say that writing a book might not be the highest and best use of your precious time. If you get through Part 1 of this book, which is about planning your business book, and you're feeling more drained than excited, that's a good reason to slow down, because even more important than writing your business book is cultivating your thought leadership ecosystem. Beyond getting the writing done, you need to ensure you have enough stamina and motivation to properly position, publish, and promote your book. This is a marathon, not a sprint.

PRE-READING EXERCISES

Now, if you know you should write your book, and you're ready to go all in, this book will show you the easiest way to fit writing a book into running your business. The tools I share will help you plan, write, and promote your book. And most important, they will simplify the process, teaching you how to prioritize your time so you don't end up overthinking where you need to let go and underthinking where you need to lean in.

I know your fingers are itching to get at that keyboard, but before you dive headlong into the rest of this book and start writing yours, I want you to pause and do some pre-reading exercises.

These exercises serve two purposes:

1. They'll affirm your belief that it really is time for you to write your business book or show you that it's not.
2. They'll get your ideas flowing with some added buy-in, which means simply by doing these exercises, you're taking action toward getting your business book written.

Selfishly, that second one matters a lot to me. I don't want this book to be "shelf-help." I hope you won't read it and then forget about it. Again, your time is valuable. So do me (and yourself) a favor and work through these pre-reading exercises. They will take less than 30 minutes.

In the end, if you're not bursting with anticipation and tripping over your own brain to get your big idea down on the page, I want you to take an honest look at whether *now* is the time to write your business book. Timing is really important. Take a lesson from me: this is actually my third attempt to write a book for myself. I have two other book manuscripts just hanging out at about 75% of the way finished somewhere in my Google Drive. So I don't want you to resist the feeling that this isn't the right idea or the right time to write your book. Trust that your idea will present itself when you're ready. Remember, you can always revisit your book idea in three months, six months, a year, or ten years. It will still be here!

On with the pre-reading exercises.

EXERCISE 1: THE CHECKLIST

The following checklist will help you determine whether you should write your business book yourself. Check all that apply.

CHECKLIST: SHOULD I WRITE MY BUSINESS BOOK MYSELF?

- ☐ I have an idea that I can't shake off.
- ☐ There are people who need to read my book.
- ☐ I can find at least 5 hours per week in my schedule for the next 16 weeks (4 months).
- ☐ I would like "book author" to be part of my identity.
- ☐ It is a dream of mine to write a book.
- ☐ Writing may not be easy, but at least it doesn't feel like quicksand.
- ☐ The idea of writing a book doesn't feel totally draining.
- ☐ Writing my own book would feel satisfying.
- ☐ Writing a book is the highest and best use of my time.
- ☐ Writing a book will further my business goals.

If you checked off at least 8 items on this list, then you should write your book. If you checked off fewer than 8, you may want to set your book to the side to revisit or consider working with a ghostwriter.

Next, brainstorm about your book idea, your book's why, and the obstacles you might face on your journey.

EXERCISE 2: MY BOOK IDEA

Set a timer for 5 minutes and freewrite about your book idea. Whether you want to grab a pen and notebook or open up your favorite digital content creation system, it doesn't matter. You can also record yourself talking about the idea on a walk or the next time you're driving—whatever works for you. I just want you to brainstorm about your idea. You can write for longer if you like, but write for at least 5 minutes.

EXERCISE 3: MY BOOK'S WHY

Chapter 2 is all about finding your book's why, but right here and now, I want you to start thinking about this. Take at least 2 minutes to answer each of the following questions (for a total of 10 minutes):

- ☐ Why do my readers need this book?
- ☐ What is the transformation my readers will undergo in reading this book?
- ☐ Why am I the one to bring this idea into the world?
- ☐ Why is now the time to start?
- ☐ What books have influenced me and shaped my journey?

EXERCISE 4: MY OBSTACLES

Finally, I want you to spend 10 minutes anticipating the obstacles you'll face when writing and promoting your book. Set a timer for 10 minutes and answer the following questions:

- ☐ What will be the hardest part?
- ☐ What are my main procrastination methods (e.g., research, distraction, hiding, imposter syndrome)?
- ☐ How will I keep moving forward when things get tough? (Ideally, come up with a few tactics that have worked for you in the past, e.g., "When I get stuck on the hardest chapter, I will break it down into smaller pieces to tackle bit by bit," or "When I feel resistance

to executing on my marketing strategy, I will find an accountability partner.")

☐ How will I recognize and manage my procrastination? (Ideally, come up with a few tactics that have worked for you in the past, e.g., "When the words aren't coming, I will take a walk around the block before coming back and writing one sentence," or "When I'm feeling vulnerable about asking people to help me promote my book, I will talk to my friend who published a book last year.")

I'd be lying if I said that I follow all of my own advice in this book, but I am making an effort to follow most of it to the extent that I would suggest that you follow it. Nothing I recommend in this book is unrealistic. I have tried to simplify the process of writing a book as much as possible. It might feel overwhelming as you read it all, but if you set a goal to take the smallest step toward planning, writing, and promoting your book every day, I think you'll feel less overwhelmed. And if that doesn't work for you, know that I won't judge you for finding your own way or "cheating" by cherry-picking the advice you want to follow. There's no cheating here—I want you to take only the advice that works for you and leave the rest without guilt.

YOU NEED A BOOK FOR YOUR BUSINESS

How did those pre-reading exercises go? Are you feeling more confident that you need to write your book? This section should strengthen your resolve. I'll tell you a bit more about myself in a moment, but one thing you should know about me is that besides being a ghostwriter, I have a PhD in philosophy. That means I can't help but think in terms of arguments. I look for justifications for everything (for better and for worse).

There are a lot of reasons why you might *want* to write a book. Maybe this idea has been percolating in your mind for years, or others have said, "You should write a book." You might believe that writing a book will make you an expert. You might believe that writing a book will gain you credibility or authority. Your best friend (or business frenemy) might have written a book, and so now you want to because of FOMO. These are not good arguments for writing a book.

Believe it or not, I talk people out of writing books (and out of hiring me to ghostwrite their books) fairly often. That's because if you don't have a business case for your book, then you shouldn't write it, no matter how badly you might want to. If you can see clearly how a book will help you grow your business, though, then you have an argument for writing a book, and you need a book for your business. If you're still reading, I probably haven't talked you out of it (yet), which is a good sign. You've made it beyond the pre-reading, which is like passing the first level of the video game. Coming up with the business case for writing your book is level two.

In Chapter 1, I ask you to make the business case for your book. That chapter is my attempt to get you to make this argument for yourself. But I also want to share what I've seen work for my clients to make the general case for why you need a book for your business.

How can a book help you grow your business? If you are running a service-based business or consultancy, growing your thought leadership should be part of your marketing strategy. You are likely running a low-volume business, where you sell premium services to fewer than 100 (or maybe even fewer than 50) clients per year. This means that you are in high demand. You also probably rely on networking and referrals rather than advertising for lead generation. Here's why you need a book for your business:

- A book can serve as marketing collateral, bringing in leads who wouldn't otherwise find you through referrals or networking.
- A book can allow you to serve people who wouldn't otherwise have access to you.
- A book can make it easier to land paid and unpaid speaking engagements that can bring in leads.
- A book boosts your authority, setting you apart as a big idea expert, and puts you at the top of your industry, which allows you to raise your fees.
- A book can become a springboard for launching other types of content (e.g., trainings, online courses, paid communities, coaching programs) that can become an additional revenue stream.

You will hear me say more than once throughout this book that you won't grow rich off of your book sales. So if you're hoping that book sales will become an additional, extremely lucrative revenue stream for you, you probably need to rethink this. Unless you write a *New York Times* bestseller, which is especially difficult to do with a business book (you would need to sell thousands of books in one week alone to even be in the running), you're not likely to make significant amounts of money from book sales. Crushing it on book sales is one side of the spectrum. On the other side is believing that you won't make any money from book sales and seeing your book as a $10 business card that you will mostly just give away. I don't want you to think of your book in this way either. I want you to look for the golden mean* between these two extremes. Aim to sell a few

---

* Aristotle examines the golden mean in Book II of the *Nicomachean Ethics*. He describes virtues of character as the mean between two extremes (vices). For example, courage is the virtue, but when taken to excess, it becomes recklessness,

thousand copies, but focus on the other ways your book can make you money. A book can help grow your business by increasing your reach, filling your pipeline, giving you the confidence to raise your prices, helping you find paid speaking opportunities, boosting sales of an online course, etc.

If any of the above, non-book-sales strategies sound like they could work for you, then you need a book for your business. But your book will grow your business only if you see it as part of your thought leadership ecosystem. This means that all of your content needs to be "rowing in the same direction." Yes, your book is a marketing tool for your business, but like all marketing tools, it requires a strategy to work. Play your cards right and your book can give you a virtually endless supply of marketing content to share, not to mention help you clarify the way you talk about your business and your brand. With the right marketing strategy around your book, you could come away thinking that your book is the single best marketing tool you've ever invested in for your business.

GET IN. GET OUT. AND GET BACK TO RUNNING YOUR BUSINESS.

Once you're convinced that you need a book for your business, how should you go about writing it? If writing a book makes sense for your business, then you want it to be as easy as possible. Again, writing a book is a sacrifice. It means you're taking time away from other business development activities you could be engaging in. It should be worth it. To me, the best way to maximize the value of your business book is to write it as quickly as possible.

---

and when someone is lacking in courage, they are described as a coward, so cowardice is the deficiency.

You can write your book in 80 days. Here are a couple of ways to do it:

1.	Write 500 words per day for 80 consecutive days	500 x 80 = 40,000 500 x 7 = 3,500 words per week 40,000 / 3,500 = 11.43 weeks
2.	Write 500 words per day, 5 days per week, for 16 weeks	500 x 80 = 40,000 500 x 5 = 2,500 words per week 40,000 / 2,500 = 16 weeks

40,000 words is a perfectly respectable goal for a business book, and 80 days is about 12 weeks, but you don't need to write for 80 consecutive days. While a lot of writers swear by writing as a daily practice, I prefer to write five days per week. In this scenario, it takes 16 weeks to get to 40,000 words.

I wrote this book even more quickly. It took me about eight weeks to get to a complete rough draft, but my big idea was seven years in the making, so it practically fell out of my brain once I sat down to write it. This is what I mean when I say that your idea may have been percolating for years before you ever sit down to write. I also want to note that I wrote the final 10,000 words in just two days while on retreat. During that writing retreat, I wrote 1,200-1,500 words during each of eight 90-minute sprints. If you can gift yourself a writing retreat, even just a weekend away by yourself, to make bigger strides with your book, I highly recommend it. I share my book timeline in Chapter 7 so you can get a feel for the whole process.

So the next question is, how long does it take you to write 500 words? I recommend working up to the point where you can write 500 words in an hour. This way, if you spend an hour writing per day, five days per week, you can get your book done in about four months. You may not write this quickly yet, so start doing some timed writing sessions to get an idea of how much time you will need. Even if it takes you six months to write your business book, this is still quite fast.

If the above sounds totally unrealistic, then I want you to ask yourself some questions:

- Are you being too precious with your writing?
- Are you putting too much pressure on yourself?
- Are you thinking of your book as something other than a marketing tool for your business?

A book is a snapshot of your brain. That's why I encourage you to write your first draft as quickly as possible. At 40,000 words, your book will be about 100-150 printed pages when it's published, which is the optimal length for a business book. This is what some refer to as an "airplane book," a book that someone could pick up and digest on a flight, in one afternoon, or over the course of one weekend. Keep in mind that your readers are busy people. They may be business owners themselves or leaders working 60 hours per week. When was the last time you met someone who had extra time on their hands every week? Your book doesn't need to be a 300-page tome.

Now, if writing your book quickly sounds like a recipe for rushing through an important project, I'm not suggesting that you cut corners. I want you to write your first messy draft quickly. I want you to write it, as much as possible, without doing any research. The point of this first draft is to get your ideas out of your head and onto the page. Then, you can take your time editing and polishing and making it your masterpiece, but if you go into the first draft with a perfectionist mindset, you will write your book agonizingly slowly. The reason I push so hard for you to get that first messy draft done is because everything gets easier once you have your full draft in front of you.

Think of yourself as painting with words. Imagine how a painter works. They first do a rough but complete pencil sketch of their subject; then they come back to paint. Now imagine how ridiculous it would be for a painter to create their piece inch by inch, sketching the upper-right-hand corner of their canvas, then painting only that part before moving on to sketch the next one-inch section of canvas. That's exactly what you're doing if you write one section or chapter and rewrite it before moving on to the next. Write the way a painter creates their work.

You will never convince me that it makes sense to spend years and years writing a business book. Get in and get out so that you can start seeing a return on the effort you put in. That's my philosophy of writing a business book. And of course, if you can't seem to break out of that perfectionist mode with your writing, there are other ways to accomplish the same goal. I've ghostwritten more than 20 books with authors who could talk about their ideas all day long but who needed someone else to put those words down on the page.

WHY THIS BOOK IS DIFFERENT

When a friend of mine suggested (forcefully) that I write a book about how to write a business book, I resisted the idea. There are so many other books out there telling you how to write a book. Does the world really need another one? Obviously, I came around to the idea, so what makes this book different?

First, most "how-to" books on writing are written by writers for other writers. You wear a lot of hats; you're a business owner, a thought leader, and an "idea" person, but one thing you are not (probably) is a writer. You need a book on writing that speaks to your unique circumstances. That's why I've written this book for you. This book is written by a business owner for other business owners.

I find that these other books spend too much time discussing the mechanics of writing when what trips up most first-time authors is not spending enough time in the ideation phase. If you're experiencing writer's block, it's probably because you haven't thought enough about your idea. It's not because you forgot the difference between an independent clause and a dependent clause (my editor can attest to the fact that I often seem to forget the difference when I'm writing).

Also, if you spend too much time overthinking the writing, you run the risk of burning yourself out before you get to the most important stuff: positioning, publishing, and promoting. What good is spending all that time writing your business book if no one reads it? As a big idea expert, you are here to share your expertise with others. Give yourself permission to write a messy first draft so that you can put more energy into talking about your big idea and shouting from the rooftops that you're writing a book.

Second, this book is designed to encourage you to write quickly, especially during the drafting phase. Your mantra should be "I will fix it in the edit." In the beginning, when your ideas are flowing, you don't want anything to get in the way of getting those ideas out onto the page. Now is not the time to be precious with your words. Again, you're trying to capture that snapshot of your brain. You literally can't f*ck this up as long as you follow where the ideas lead you.

The other advantage of writing quickly is that it defangs the writing process. Writing can feel intimidating, especially to nonwriters and first-time authors. Getting out of your own way means proving your inner critic wrong, and the best way to do that is to get that messy first draft finished. It's natural to feel fear the first time you do something. Remember, fear is often a sign that you are onto something great; we feel fear whenever we step out of our comfort zone. So thank your inner critic for trying to keep you safe, and let them know that you've got this.

The third way this book is different is that it encourages you to bring in collaboration wherever possible. This is what your English teachers probably didn't teach you about writing. So many think of writing as a solitary pursuit. There's the image we have in our heads of the scribe with a long beard, sitting alone, cup of tea in hand, holed up in his candlelit room, hunched over his desk for hours, only emerging once his manuscript is complete. Writing is much more fun and fulfilling, however, when we seek feedback from others, discuss our process, and lean on friends for support when we run into roadblocks. Find others with whom you can share your half-baked ideas. Your business book will be better for it.

WHO THE HELL AM I, ANYWAY?

Earlier I promised that I'd tell you a bit more about myself. I am the owner of The Pocket PhD and the ghostwriter for renegades. I help thought leaders turn their big ideas into business books. My team and I collaborate with subject matter experts and fringe entrepreneurs to cultivate their thought leadership ecosystem, a system of interdependent content pieces (short- and long-form) connected by a dynamic strategy, which takes into account tone, distribution, audience, and business goals. When I'm not writing intensely, I'm most likely practicing yoga intensely.

As a ghostwriter, I have developed a process for writing books that improves with each client. While every book project is different, it's always important to meet with a client and capture their unique voice. For this reason, collaboration is the centerpiece of our work together. Meeting with my clients weekly, I take their book from outline to complete manuscript in 16 weeks. To accomplish this, I work on only one book at a time so I can immerse myself in each project.

The first milestone of my ghostwriting process is to get the complete, messy first draft finished in eight weeks, leaving eight more weeks to do two rounds of revisions. See, I'm giving you 16 weeks to write your first draft. That's double what I give myself when I'm writing for my clients. How generous of me. So you can trust me when I say nothing I'm sharing in this book is unrealistic.

In the rest of this book, I take you behind the curtain and give you a glimpse inside my ghostwriting process. You likely won't be able to write your book the way I write for my clients (though I'll never be one to hold you back). The distance I have from the information I pull out of my clients gives me a distinct advantage. Still, if you follow my advice, you can write the first draft of your book in 80 days. Getting it done is all about avoiding the pitfalls that many seem to fall into, obstacles like:

- Not leaning on others for support
- Not having done enough ideation
- Not making the book a true priority
- Not writing through the writer's block
- Not realizing how much thinking happens during the writing process
- Not letting that first messy draft out of your head

RADICAL TRUST

The final thing I want you to remember as you embark on this journey to getting your manuscript written is that success is all about figuring out when to let go of control and lean into trust. Because you are in a symbiotic relationship with your idea, you can trust that it will lead you where you need to go. And this is an act of radical trust.

I know this sounds kind of "woo-woo," but anyone who has engaged in the creative process knows that surrendering is the key to finishing a creative project. You have to trust yourself and your idea enough to let go of control. If you try to grip your way through the whole writing process, you will lose your nerve, or maybe you'll finish your book feeling so burned out that you don't even want to look at it again. And the price of overthinking the writing is that you will underthink everything else, and the "everything else" actually determines whether your book is a success. It's important to trust yourself and your idea so that you can relax, enjoy the process, and write the best book you can within the constraints you have.

I realize that it's easy for me to say, "Trust your idea," "Trust the process," and it's not at all easy to do. One of the things that helps, though, is finding a support system that can serve as your hype team. I'm serious. You need to connect with those who will lift you up and pump you up so you can not only get through the first draft but also do the marketing that will introduce you to the world as the big idea expert you are. When you don't believe in yourself, your support system can stand in the gap and help you stay on track.

In the spirit of balancing trust and control, I begin each of the three parts of this book with a common trap that authors fall into.

TRAP #1: DOING TOO MUCH PLANNING

First, planning your book is important. But you probably need less planning time than you think. Exhibit 1: When I started writing this book, I planned to spend six months coming up with my book idea; instead, a friend pointed out that I already had my book idea, and this book fell out of my brain in two months. Planning can become a procrastination mechanism. So the trap to avoid at this stage is doing too much planning. Trust that you've been preparing to write this book from day one of your business, if not longer.

TRAP #2: OVERTHINKING THE WRITING

Once you get to the writing stage, the trap to avoid is overthinking the writing and seeing your book as a credential. You can freeze up here if you insist on maintaining too much control while you write. Instead, think about only one thing: getting to the end of your messy first draft as quickly as you can. Set your weekly word count goal and be relentless about sticking to it (allow for some trial and error in the beginning, but once you get into a groove, be relentless about staying in that groove). Again, I recommend aiming for 500 words five days per week.

It's also important during the full-on writing phase to remember that your book might not unfold in a linear way. When we first start writing, we believe the process will look like this:

- Outline my book
- Write each part of the outline in order, starting with the introduction and ending with the conclusion
- Complete my draft

In reality, you might move back and forth between each of these steps in all kinds of ways. You might think you have a complete outline, but once you start writing, realize you need to add additional chapters. You might have a complete outline and then, once you start writing, realize it needs to be reorganized. You might struggle to write your outline, so you decide to just dive in and start writing. You might jump around from chapter to chapter to hit your word count goal each day. All of this is natural and perfect.

TRAP #3: UNDERTHINKING THE POSITIONING, PUBLISHING, AND PROMOTING

Finally, in the final stage, positioning, publishing, and promoting, the big trap to avoid is believing that you've finished the marathon once your book is written. You need to leave some gas in the tank so that you can market your book without cutting corners. In fact, it's smart to think about positioning while you write and to start promoting at least three months before your publication date. This means that even before you finish your messy first draft, you should have an idea of how your book is unique so that your book can speak to that.

These big three traps can be summed up as overthinking the writing and underthinking everything else. When you find yourself getting bogged down in the writing, when that inner critic starts chirping at you, employ one of two strategies: ignore those thoughts and keep writing or shift to writing your marketing plan or executing on it. If you do this every time, you will keep moving forward.

There may be other traps that tempt you too. As you discover them, write them down and brainstorm ways you can avoid them or wriggle out of them in the future. Remember, the writing process is a work in progress. You won't "solve" these traps once and for all. You will need to stay vigilant throughout to ensure that you're staying on track.

HOW TO READ THIS BOOK

Like the book-writing process, this book is deceptively linear. It's easy to think that when you're in the planning phase, you should read Part 1. When you're ready for the writing phase, you should read Part 2. And when your manuscript is complete and ready for publishing, then you should read Part 3. But this is not the best way to read this book. It's also not the best way to approach your writing process. In particular, you should be thinking about positioning and promoting while you write your first draft. And you should start marketing your book at least three months out from your book launch date, though it's never too early to start talking about your book and sharing your half-baked ideas—yes, I know it's scary, but the earlier you share your ideas, the more time you have to polish them or scrap them if they don't resonate. So if you're less than three months out from your book launch today, I encourage you to skip ahead and read the third part on publishing, positioning, and promoting first.

The best approach to reading this book is to consider where you are in the process and dive into the parts where you have questions. More than a few times, it has crossed my mind that I should have written this book as a *Choose Your Own Adventure*. Depending on where you are in the process, it's more useful for you to start at one particular point and work your way through, choosing the fork that best applies to your own situation or problem. I've done my best to add cross-references to different chapters wherever it makes sense and to help you make this book your own in some sense.

The next best approach is to read through this book cover to cover before you start writing or when you're in the early stages of writing. This will give you the lay of the land and some food for thought as you prepare. Think of it as your guide to planning out your book writing process. It will help you anticipate decisions to make and when to make them. Also, consider that plans are only really useful when you operationalize them.* This is a lesson I keep learning over and over in my business. If I don't take the time to break my plans down and add those smaller steps to my task management system, I won't execute on my plans. Use the parts of this book to think about how

---

* I learned this lesson from my wonderful fractional COO, Podge Thomas (https://smallbusinesscopilot.io), who helps me to operationalize all of my plans in Notion. I highly recommend working with her and using Notion to keep track of your book writing progress.

to operationalize your book writing plan. It wouldn't hurt for you to reread this book after you've finished your draft too, especially Part 3, or to revisit certain sections as you go through your journey.

A NOTE ON THE TITLE

Unwritten may seem like an odd title for a book about writing a book. It's meant to be tongue-in-cheek. First, it's a nod to my work as a ghostwriter. See, as a ghostwriter, my clients are exactly the kind of people who want to write a book without having to write it themselves. This is what ghostwriting is all about—transforming unwritten ideas into written ones. It's what ghostwriters are for.

Second, when you're writing a book, it's easy to focus on the fact that it's unwritten and to feel like you need to apologize for not being further along. So I hope the title serves as a reminder that there's no shame in your book being unwritten. "Unwritten" is a necessary stage on the way to having been written. Trust your idea. Trust the process.

Also, *Unwritten* serves as a reminder that having a book is not what makes you an expert. You're already an expert, though you might have some trouble owning your expertise. Your expertise is unwritten, which should help you feel free to express it. As Natasha Bedingfield says, "Today is where your book begins / The rest is still unwritten."*

---

* Natasha Bedingfield, vocalist, "Unwritten," 2004, by Natasha Bedingfield (lyricist), Danielle Brisebois (lyricist), and Wayne Rodrigues (lyricist), vol 1, track 4, on *Unwritten* (New York: Epic Records), 2005.

Part 1

WHERE TO BEGIN

When it comes to finding the easiest way to fit writing a book into running your business, it starts even before you write your first sentence. How you approach planning to write your book tells you everything you need to know about how the writing process will go for you. This means if you know you have a tendency to overthink the writing and underthink everything else about this process, I want you to consider how you can flip this switch in your brain starting *now*.

If you didn't do the pre-reading exercises in the introduction, go back and do those now. I wrote those exercises specifically as a warm-up to Part 1 to help you get into the proper mindset. Short bursts of ideation and writing sessions with time limits are a great tool to get you moving and keep you from indulging too much in the planning process.

WHAT'S YOUR WRITER PERSONA?

Writers sometimes talk about different writer personas. There are the Planners, who think planning is the best part of the writing process. Planners love a good outline and are most likely to rewrite an outline (perhaps several times) before they even think about starting the rough draft. They may even delight in creating Pinterest boards envisioning their ideal writing space and devote hours to finding the perfect scented candle for creative inspiration.

Contrast this with the Sprinters (sometimes called Pantsers), who prefer to write "by the seat of their pants." When Sprinters sit down to write, their goal is to get in and get out as quickly as possible. They don't have much (if any) patience for planning, and they see writing merely as a tool for expressing their best ideas.

As a recovering Planner myself, I have learned to flip that switch in my brain. When I wrote philosophy papers as a graduate student and later as a professor, I was a serious Planner. I always spent the bulk of my time outlining and re-outlining until the outline felt perfect. My outlines were often several pages long and closer to handwritten rough drafts in the end (part of the reason for this might be that I wrote most of my papers in college by hand before trekking to the computer lab to type them up). Looking back, I did this because outlining was my way of ideating. In my outline, I was thinking and plotting out each idea I was stringing together. But it was a painfully slow process that perpetuated a perfectionist mindset. And it led to an equally painfully slow writing and rewriting process where I worked to perfect nearly every sentence until the deadline dictated I had to stop.

If you also tend more toward the Planner side of things, you need to watch out for the trap of overplanning.

TRAP #1: DOING TOO MUCH PLANNING

Before you even start writing your book, you could run into this big obstacle. As a big idea expert, it's very possible that you tend toward overthinking. And you need to look out for the risk that you will spend too much time planning. You may love to luxuriate in mind mapping, outlining, and imagining your perfect writing space. You may get lost down rabbit holes trying to find just the right app to help you plot out every square inch of your book. And it's okay to indulge in your own tendencies to a certain extent. After all, this process should be enjoyable—and satisfying, remember?

Still, if you find yourself using planning as a procrastination mechanism to avoid writing, that's when you need to cut yourself off and start hacking away at the elephant (aka your book).*

Earlier I said I used to be much more of a Planner. Entrepreneurship has changed me in a lot of ways, but perhaps the most obvious shift is how it has molded me into an action taker. In my business, I discovered how much taking action helped me get beyond my fear and step outside of my comfort zone. Now, if anything, I err on the side of taking action too quickly. But I think this is the best side of the pendulum for me to be on.†

---

* Desmond Tutu once said, "There's only one way to eat an elephant: a bite at a time." What he meant is that everything in life that seems daunting or even impossible, like writing your book, can be accomplished by taking small steps. Of course, this only works if you get started. You have to move beyond the planning stage and take action.

† Going back to Aristotle's golden mean, he also thought that if you tended toward one vice, you should actually try to overshoot the mean

This general orientation toward action-taking has definitely affected my writer persona. Since I started my business, I've turned over a whole new leaf (or perhaps I've rediscovered my true nature). I have become a full-fledged Sprinter. I realize now that creating long, detailed outlines is usually a waste of time. (Of course, business writing is a whole different beast from academic writing. Still, I think that creating long, detailed outlines is usually little more than an overindulgence, regardless of the type of writing you're doing.) The result is better—the content more balanced—when I start with a high-level outline or mind map and do most of my ideating as I'm writing my first draft. My goal is really to get in and get out with a messy first draft ASAP. This is the process I use to write my clients' first drafts in eight weeks, the process I used to write this book, and the process I recommend for you as you write your business book.

I also adore collaborative writing (and wish there were more room for this type of writing in academia). As soon as I feel stuck, instead of trying to write myself out of the hole I've dug, I reach out to someone in my support system and ask them for feedback. Not only does talking through my thoughts ensure that I don't stay stuck for long, but it also allows me to test, refine, and expand my ideas as I'm writing.

So Part 1 is all about helping you avoid the trap of over-planning and get to writing your way to the finish line (Part 2).

---

by aiming at the opposite vice, and then you would end up hitting it dead on. It's like shooting an arrow at a bull's-eye when there's a strong wind. You want to aim into the wind.

Chapter 1

WHAT'S THE BUSINESS CASE FOR YOUR BOOK?

One of the first questions I ask every book ghostwriting prospect who agrees to a discovery call with me is "What's the business case for your book?"

When you're writing a business book, you are taking time away from other revenue-generating tasks, so it needs to be clear to you why you are doing this. If writing your book is not the highest and best use of your time, then you shouldn't write it. Period.

Also, it's important to keep in mind that there are seasons to building a business. Writing a book needs to align with the season you're in. This means, for example, if you have an immediate need to generate revenue for your business, writing a book should wait. A business book can and will generate revenue for you, but not immediately. So the time may not be right for you to write your book. I know this might feel like a hard pill to swallow. But if you are just starting your business (i.e., less than three years in), focused on fundraising for a start-up, or looking to scale your business, wait to write your book. It will be an easier process, more satisfying, and a better book if you wait. So if you're not sure whether now is the right time, ask yourself, "What's the business case for my book?"

Can you write a book because you want to add "author" to your LinkedIn headline? Can you write a book to leave a legacy for your grandkids? Can you write a book because you have an incredible story that the world needs to hear? Can you write a book to help you heal from your trauma and share important lessons you've learned? Yes. Yes. Yes. And yes. But I want to make this clear: the advice I share in this book doesn't apply if you aren't writing a book primarily for the purpose of cultivating your thought leadership ecosystem, and if you are writing a book for this reason, then it needs to be clear to you how this book will make you money.

HINT: YOU WON'T MAKE MONEY ON BOOK SALES

The primary source of revenue you receive from your book will not be from book sales. If this is breaking news for you, I'm sorry to shatter your dream of seeing your book on Reese Witherspoon's book club list. But I want you to go into this with your eyes wide open, so let's look at some numbers. In 2021, 2.3 million books were self-published in the U.S., and 2021 is the third year in a row that more than 2 million books were self-published.[*] As for traditional publishing, according to one industry estimate, 500,000 to 1 million new book titles are published each year.[†] That means a combined 3 million books are published each year in the U.S. alone. Yet book sales have remained flat for the past 20 years. The average book published today, across all categories of fiction and nonfiction, sells fewer than 300 print copies

---

[*] *Publishers Weekly*, February 20, 2023.

[†] Dean Talbot, "Number of Books Published per Year," *WordsRated*, February 2, 2022.

over its lifetime,* and the average price for a nonfiction, hardcover book in 2022 was $28.97.† I'll let you do the math on that to see why I'm not optimistic about getting rich off of book sales as a business book author (and authors don't even get to keep 100% of the royalties). And even if we include e-book sales, audio sales, sales outside of the U.S., and sales outside of retail channels, the average book is selling fewer than 1,000 copies over its lifetime in all formats and all markets.‡

The reality is that it's very difficult to get an advance from a publisher or make significant sales of a business book unless you have already built up quite a following (e.g., publishers look for a minimum of 10,000 LinkedIn followers). If you're focused on book sales, ask yourself whether you think you have what it takes to be in the top 1% of authors—and I'm not talking about the quality of your content. I'm talking about earning a spot in the top 1% of nonfiction book sales. If the answer is yes, then you should be laser-focused on building your following before you write your book. In our content-(over)saturated world, it's simply not true that the books that sell more than 300 copies have the highest quality content. However, there are plenty of other reasons to write an incredible book besides book sales.

WHAT A BOOK CAN DO FOR YOUR BUSINESS

So if you won't make money selling copies of your book, how will you make money? A business book—even if you give away more copies

---

* The 10 Awful Truths about Book Publishing, updated March 1, 2023 (https://ideas.bkconnection.com/10-awful-truths-about-publishing).

† Average Book Prices for 2022 (https://s3.us-east-1.amazonaws.com/WebVault/SLJ/EDIT22/PDF/Avg-Book-Prices-Full-Chart-2022.pdf).

‡ The 10 Awful Truths about Book Publishing, updated March 1, 2023 (https://ideas.bkconnection.com/10-awful-truths-about-publishing).

than you sell—can give your business a significant boost. It can increase your authority as the go-to thought leader in your industry. It can help you more fully own your expertise, which can lead to opportunities you may not even be able to anticipate. It can be a lead-generation tool, a sales tool, and a conversation starter. It can help you reach a broader audience and spread the word about your work. In short, it makes you a big idea expert.

All of these possibilities are real, but I haven't yet shown you the money. You're wondering how any of the above will lead to dollars in the bank (good!). If you do any business through referrals, then being the go-to thought leader in your industry is huge. Sure, people who know you well will refer you. They'll do so even if you don't publish a book, because they recognize your expertise. But consider how many people know you well.

You can do this as an exercise: write down a list of business contacts who you would say know you well and whom you could see sending you referrals. In my world, I can only think of maybe 20 or 30 people who I would say know me well and are great referral sources. Now, when I think of how often each of those people encounters someone who needs a ghostwriter and is a good fit for me, it's easy to see that the number of referrals from people who know me well might top out at ten in a good year.

Now consider what happens when I write a book and become the go-to business book ghostwriter. Suddenly people who don't know me well but who find themselves in need of a referral to share are much more likely to find my name or think of me. Instead of 20 or 30 people referring me, I now have hundreds or thousands of people who feel comfortable referring me because they see that I've written a book in my area of expertise. Every reader becomes a potential referral source, and I've gained their trust without having to really get to know them. Keep in mind I'm only talking about one of the benefits a book can bring. Each new opportunity has the potential to add new referral partners to your network.

Should every business owner have a book? Absolutely not. In fact, there are likely more reasons not to write a book than reasons to write a book. A book is one potential revenue generator in your business, and you have to make decisions about the best revenue generators for your business. That's what tips the balance in your favor. I meet entrepreneurs all the time who are less than three years into running their businesses and excited to tell me about their book ideas. I always tell them to wait. I don't like to go around raining on people's parades, but as an ex of mine used to say to me when I complained about him raining on my parade, "Am I raining on your parade? Or are you throwing a parade in the rain?" Don't throw a parade in the rain. In those early years, you need time to identify and test your business model, build your systems and protocols, and decide what works. You do not need to add book writing to all that chaos. Trust me. You'll write a better book if you wait. So one reason not to write a book is because you are too early in your business, but there are many other reasons why it doesn't make sense.

Here is a checklist to help you decide if you have a case for writing your business book.

CHECKLIST: HOW DOES THE BOOK FIT INTO YOUR BUSINESS AS A WHOLE? CHECK ALL THAT APPLY.

- ☐ I want to use my book to land paid and unpaid speaking gigs.
- ☐ I want to use my book to sell an existing online course or training.
- ☐ I want to use my book as a companion to an online course or training I will create.

☐ I want to use my book to drive traffic to my website.
☐ I want to use my book as a springboard to building thought leadership.
☐ I want to use my book to increase my consulting fees.
☐ I want to use my book to reach a new or broader audience.

The more of these boxes you check off, the stronger your business case for writing your book. Remember, whether you should write your book yourself is a separate question from whether you have a business case for writing your book. Return to the checklist in the introduction if you're wondering whether it makes sense to write your book yourself.

RESULTS

Talking about a business case for your book goes beyond connecting the dots between your book and other revenue-generating activities. Yes, a book will generate leads not only for your products and services but also for more indirect ways of growing your business (e.g., speaking, consulting, and ideation). I've ghostwritten or edited more than 20 books. For my clients who have been most successful, they came to me with a clear goal in mind. Here are some of the results they've seen:

- Sold more than 1,000 copies in the first year after publication, primarily by promoting on LinkedIn
- Created a course after writing the book, using the book as an outline for the course
- Used the book as an add-on and incentive for clients to buy a course or program

- Shifted from delivering services primarily one-on-one to delivering services to groups
- Expanded their client base
- Expanded their referral network
- Landed paid speaking gigs
- Used the book as a way to uplevel their PR game
- Were able to increase their fees because the book increased demand for their services

In later chapters, I'll come back to these results and talk about the exact methods used to realize those goals. It all starts with your book's "why."

Chapter 2

YOUR BOOK'S WHY

If you've started a business within the past 20 years, you are likely familiar with Simon Sinek's idea about starting with your big why. He introduced the idea in his 2009 book, *Start with Why: How Great Leaders Inspire Everyone to Take Action,* but I first encountered the concept in 2014, when a mentor shared his 2010 TED Talk, which happens to be one of the most-viewed TED Talks of all time.

I started The Pocket PhD in 2015 after I got chewed up and spit out by the soul-crushing machine that is the academic job market. Buy me a glass of wine (or just ask me) and I'll tell you some of my war stories. But when I leaped out of the ivory tower and flew into the business world, I couldn't have a conversation about my business without someone bringing up Simon Sinek or asking, "What's your why?"

By the way, Sinek is a good example of a subject matter expert who transformed into a big idea expert. And I can see why Sinek's big idea had legs. It's a simple concept that's easy to grasp. It's relatable

and applicable to household brands. It's memorable and a good conversation starter to use at a networking event or a cocktail party. Plus,
starting with your "why" or your deeper purpose speaks to the entre-
preneurial desire to do work that's meaningful and to free yourself
from the red tape that comes with working for someone else. "What's
your why?" is the perfect question to start a movement and become
an anthem for business owners. If your book idea is like this, then you
will easily sell more than 300 copies with the right marketing and
promotional strategy.

Finding your why can be intrinsically motivating too. It gives your
business something to anchor into. On the days when you're thinking
about burning it all to the ground and going to work digging ditches,
you can remind yourself why you're putting yourself through the
wringer, and it gives you the push you need to keep going.

You need the same kind of intrinsic motivation to get your book
across the finish line. Note that your book's why is different from asking you, the author, why you're writing this book—just like Simon
Sinek isn't asking entrepreneurs about their businesses' origin stories.
I'm asking you to connect with the deeper meaning guiding you to
write this book and connecting you with your ideal reader.

Your book's why is related to your reader's transformation. Here's
a quick exercise to help you find your book's why.

EXERCISE: FINDING YOUR BOOK'S WHY

Before your reader is aware of your book, they are at point A. Describe
point A. After they read your book, they'll find themselves at point B.
Describe point B. Your book is the bridge to get them from point A to
point B. Taking readers on this journey is your book's why.

Your book's why could also be about you. Perhaps you're writing
to a younger version of yourself in the hopes that you can help those

who find themselves in the same place avoid certain mistakes. You might feel that your purpose is to pass on the lessons you learned the hard way, and now you are on a mission to make others' lives easier or even change how things are done in your industry. Notice, though, that this also ties back to the reader's transformation. In this case, you experienced the same transformation you're now guiding others to go through.

Your book's why could also be about the idea itself. You have a big, hairy, audacious idea that you can't shake off. If you didn't, then you wouldn't even be thinking about writing a book. What would happen if everyone who matters adopted your way of thinking? How would the world change? The answer to these questions could be your book's why. Again, I'm asking you to consider the transformation your book catalyzes.

My book's why: To make the case to business owners, who aren't natural writers but who are big idea people, that writing a book is for them. At point A, my readers have an idea that they can't shake off, but they're not sure if they have what it takes to bring it into the world. They don't know if they should make the sacrifice. At point B, my readers are big idea experts. They see themselves in a symbiotic relationship with their idea. They are no longer overthinking the writing. And they understand the importance of positioning, publishing, and promoting their business book. They know that their unwritten ideas want to come into the world and believe that they are the ones to shepherd those ideas. They see themselves as the copilots of their ideas (with apologies for the mixed metaphor, though I see no reason why shepherds can't also be copilots).

Now it's your turn to think about your book's why. What's the transformation you want your reader to make? Once you find your book's why, write it down somewhere, and post it in a place where you can see it whenever you work on your book.

CONNECTING WITH YOUR AUDIENCE

Your book's why is about connecting to your purpose in getting your big, hairy, audacious idea out of your head and into the world. You want to think about connecting with your audience as well.

When I started writing this book, I thought I was just writing it for myself. This is because I was buying into an assumption that a lot of people make about ghostwriters—that since the writing we do is confidential and under someone else's name, we feel bad because we don't "get credit" for our work. For a moment, I bought into the shame-based thought that I needed to write a book for myself instead of "giving my superpower away." Although this isn't at all how I see the work I do with my clients, I had internalized some of these judgments, and I thought that writing my own book would help me "prove" that I'm as much of a big idea expert as my clients.

Then someone reminded me that connecting with my audience would also give me a lot of motivation. I'm not really writing this book for myself. If I were, then there would be no real reason to publish it. Merely writing the draft would accomplish my goal. Actually, I'm writing this book for the business owner who is struggling to write their book or wondering if writing a book is even a thing they should be spending time, energy, and money on. Connecting to these people (many of whom I've already met as I talk about writing this book) helps me keep moving forward. When we think about and empathize with our readers, we start to get a really good picture of who we're writing to and why they need to read our book. And if we really connect with them, down to picturing one person in particular reading our book, then we feel a drive to get the book done for that person.

To connect with your audience, think about who you're writing to. If it's your former self, then it should be easy to connect with your reader. If it's a client you're picturing, think about one of your actual clients and write your book for them. This is a tip I learned when I first started writing blog articles for entrepreneurs. Whenever you're writing any type of content, imagine writing to one person in particular rather than some amorphous mass of an audience. Simply imagining yourself in conversation with one person will bring your writing to life.

You can also connect to your audience by doing some research into your target reader, if it feels right. This works best if you can get specific feedback. You could come up with a list of three to five questions, for example, and actually interview people who are in your target audience. You could do a focus group. Or you could spend some time engaging with your target readers online or during in-person networking events. An easy, low-maintenance way to do market research is, whenever you meet someone who seems like they could be a good fit, have a few questions at the ready. You'll be amazed at how feedback from others will influence the direction of your book in a really positive way.

Here are some potential audience connection questions:

- When you think of [your book's main topic], what first comes to mind?
- Have you ever considered [one of your book's recommendations]? Why or why not?
- Where have you struggled the most with [your topic or subtopic]?
- What are your favorite resources for [your topic or subtopic]?

You can also share a puzzle, obstacle, pain point, or trap that is motivating you and ask whether it resonates with them.

WHAT BOOKS HAVE INFLUENCED YOU?

Another good place to start when it comes to getting ready to write your book is with the books (and other writings) that have influenced you. Now, I'm not suggesting that you pore over some books, taking painstaking notes about what you like most (I've done this, and it isn't that helpful). Instead, set a timer for five minutes and write down all the books that come to mind (you may have already started this list with the pre-reading exercises). Sure, you'll want to think about the most influential business books you've read, but you'll also want to include novels, memoirs, science fiction, etc. Whatever surfaces is a fine book to add to the list.

Now look at your list, and for each book, write down what stuck with you. What do you remember? What did you like? Then think about how you might incorporate or draw on these ideas as you write your book. Keep an open mind here. Something like excellent character development might not seem like it relates to writing a business book, but if you dig deeper, you may find that an author's skill at character development can teach you something about writing case studies, client success stories, or explaining one of your processes in the book.

The business books on your list can help you determine what you want your general tone to be. Do you like books with chapters that start out explaining or teaching a lesson before moving into an example to illustrate? Or do you prefer books that weave stories throughout? Do you prefer longer chapters or shorter chapters? What types of graphics, illustrations, and exercises enhance your experience? And if there are no business books on your list, then that's something to consider too.

Also, think about this as you read new stuff too. If you're like me, you'll probably be primed to think about writing while you're reading (it's actually one of the hazards of being a writer—though to be honest, thinking about the author's writing process enhances the reading experience for me).

Taking the time to analyze the books that have most influenced you as a reader will help you make decisions about what will be most helpful for your readers. Above all, make sure that you're not over-thinking the planning process. The crown jewel of the whole process is writing your book. Don't burn yourself out at this stage.

Chapter 3

WHAT KIND OF BOOK ARE YOU WRITING?

Once you have an idea about your book's why (and the main topic—which is hopefully coming into focus after the pre-reading exercises), which you're going to explore in your book, it's time to think about the best way to package up your idea. If you have been wondering about this, that's a great sign because it shows that you're focused on strategy, which is just where I want you to be. How you choose to package your book idea could be related to positioning, which is something I discuss in Part 3. Here I want to ask a simpler question: What kind of book are you writing?

Now, this book is not just about helping you get across the finish line. It's also about cultivating your thought leadership ecosystem. And this relates to what we talked about back in Chapter 1, the business case for your book. So before you decide what type of book you are writing, you need to think a bit about where your book fits into your thought leadership ecosystem.

For example, here is the pattern I see most often with the clients I work with:

- They publish a book, which contains basically everything they know about a particular topic (e.g., best practices for communicating about organizational change), including the results they can expect to see if readers follow the advice shared.
- People inside and outside of the organizational development community buy the book, read the book, and then realize communicating about change management is way more complicated than they first thought.
- Because readers-turned-prospects don't believe they can achieve those results themselves and because my client's book has positioned them as a thought leader, readers-turned-prospects call my client and hire them to create a communications strategy.

In other words, a business book can be an important lead-generation strategy. Earlier I talked about how having a book can increase the number of unofficial referral partners you have in your network. Well, it turns out that this is only one way your book can generate leads for your business. It can also serve as a more direct lead magnet.

As a leader, expert, or consultant, you might worry about giving away too much in your book. (I know I have worried about this myself. Why would a ghostwriter give away their best secrets for writing a book?) But the reality is that the more you share, the more your readers start to wonder if this is something they really want to or can do for themselves. *And* you've just cleared one of the biggest hurdles in the sales cycle: you've proven to them that you know your sh*t and have gained their trust. As long as they're ready to solve the problem and looking to make the transformation your book offers, they are primed to sign the contract. Hiring you is the "easy button."

So the big question to answer in this chapter is, What is the best type of book to serve as the vehicle to showcase your thought leadership?

WHAT IS THE BEST TYPE OF BOOK TO SHOWCASE YOUR THOUGHT LEADERSHIP?

Successful business books fall into one of three buckets: the how-to book, the interview book, and the business memoir. Let's take a closer look at each.

1. THE HOW-TO BOOK

It's easiest to see how this type of book fits with the lead-generation pattern I described above. In a how-to book, you basically describe your process for working with your clients to deliver the results they're after.

The how-to book is often structured as X steps to achieve Y result (e.g., 10 Steps to Building the Consulting Practice of Your Dreams). Here, you're teaching your readers how to do something using your unique process. If you own a service-based business and work with one-on-one clients, writing a how-to book could be a good choice because you likely have a clear process that you take your clients through and particular skills that you want to teach them. All you have to do is write down your process and the skills, and *voilà*, you have your book.

This is perhaps the easiest choice for getting your book done in 80 days. You can literally take notes during your next client engagement, gather all the documents and tech you use with each client, and have the start of a great business book.

How-to books also usually include some examples to illustrate different steps in the process. Client examples are a great addition to

any process-oriented book. These real-world examples help make
the process clearer for nonexperts. So you'll also want to take notes
and gather evidence of client results that you can share in your book.
If you're concerned at all about confidentiality, you can anonymize
your examples or simply ask your clients for permission to use their
story.

When I work with my ghostwriting clients, I often ask them to
explain to me how they work with their clients. Getting those specifics
really helps me to wrap my brain around their methodology, and the
same will be true of your readers.

You will likely want to weave in elements from your own story
too. Your readers will appreciate a look "behind the curtain" at your
process. They will enjoy geeking out with you, so don't be afraid to
dig deep, answering questions like:

- How did you arrive at this process?
- Can you talk about the trial and error it took to get here?
- Do you have a humorous anecdote to share about what
  happens if someone skips a step?
- Is there a step that you used to include, but now you
  don't for some reason?
- Have you always included all of these steps in your pro-
  cess? What made you change your process or add to it?

2. THE INTERVIEW BOOK

Writing an interview book can be another super quick and easy way
to get your book done. This type of book is best for advanced topics
rather than a basic-level business book. If you're an expert who enjoys
talking shop with other experts and who knows a lot of other experts,
especially "heavy hitters" who could help to put your name on the

map (or you're looking for a good reason to connect with experts in your field), then you may want to go for an interview book. This is obviously a great choice if you have a podcast too.

The bulk of the content in this type of book comes from interviews with experts, which all relate to a certain topic. The biggest challenge here is filling in the content between interviews to make sure everything links together in a cohesive way. It helps if you have your own angle on the topic that you want to push. This way you can develop a framework through which to filter the information you receive from your interviewees.

For example, if you want to interview consultants in your field to talk about best practices, make sure that you have some strong opinions of your own. This way, when you find a point of disagreement, it can be fodder for conversation and healthy debate, which can turn into helpful content for your readers.

I've seen authors make the mistake of not really having an agenda other than to interview a bunch of people in their area of expertise and then trying to find a common thread and construct a narrative after the fact. This could work—if you're lucky—but it's going to be a lot easier to come up with a clear structure, then create questions to help you fill in the gaps within your narrative. There's no reason to fear steering your interviewees in your direction. Objectivity is great in science and politics, but as an expert writing a business book, realize that your readers are coming to you to hear what you think based on your experience, and lean into this as an advantage.

Even if you have in mind an introductory book to your industry with best practices, don't simply go out and ask other experts about best practices. Instead, choose something that's not accepted as doctrine in your field. What's a bit controversial? What might get experts' engines turning when they sit down for an interview with you? This will give you a more interesting result.

Remember, you're in control of your book. If you don't have a clear agenda, you risk allowing others to steer you in a direction that's not most advantageous for you. Since your book is as much marketing for your business as a piece of content that needs to be marketed in its own right, you must keep in mind what will create the highest and best value within this specific context.

3. THE BUSINESS MEMOIR

The third "bucket" of business books I want to talk about is the memoir. A memoir is a nonfiction account of some portion of a person's life told from the perspective of the author, but the business memoir differs from other types of memoirs. In a business memoir, the personal story ties into a business lesson or message of some kind. In fact, the business lesson should take center stage.

There's of course, nothing wrong with writing a memoir without a business lesson. If you're a celebrity or a politician or have accomplished something less than 1% of the population has accomplished—or you can imagine your story on the big screen—you can write about your life without worrying much about whether there's a business lesson there. Because your story has legs by itself, you can let others draw their own lessons (oh, and you likely have an audience champing at the bit to buy anything you publish). However, as an entrepreneur, you'll want to think about how the memoir elements of your book enhance the big message. Having a great story to tell is helpful, but it will only take you so far.

Since you're focused on the business case for your book, your book needs to fit within your thought leadership ecosystem. So everything you write should be viewed through that lens. If you're writing about how, for example, a traumatic moment in your life helped you to see your clients differently, you will want to lead with talking about your clients and the work that you do. Writing a business memoir means masterfully weaving in the personal story with the business lessons in such a way that the reader never gets bored with one narrative. The interplay between the two narratives can be a good way to help your readers stay focused.

Most of the business books I've written with my clients have included elements of memoir. Readers connect with personal stories, so no matter what type of book you choose to write, you'll want to include moments of vulnerability and stories that your reader can relate to on an emotional level. It's difficult to give general advice about how to make this work. Follow your instincts when it comes to writing about your life and seeing how it fits into your business.

WHICH TYPE OF BOOK SHOULD I WRITE?

I have written and edited all three types of books. There's no single right answer for which type is better than another, and any of the three can be adapted to meet any business goal. The best type of book for you to write is the one that you feel most confident writing and that will showcase your big idea best.

Consider what type of book your readers most want to read, what type of book you most like to read, and what type of book sounds the most exciting for you to write. Here are some frameworks my clients have used:

- A how-to book sharing a particular methodology about how to design an online course. The book walks readers through all the necessary elements and skills needed to create an online course or training, along with providing many examples from real courses illustrating each step.
- An interview book created by a consultant for other consultants just starting out in a specialized field. The

book introduces readers to the author's framework and features highlights from interviews with 20 consultants to support key points made throughout the book.

- A memoir from a tech entrepreneur about how he built and scaled his first start-up. Without taking a dime of venture capital or seeking out investor funding, he bootstrapped the company, selling it to a big competitor for a multimillion-dollar payout.

Chapter 4

OVERCOMING OBSTACLES TO WRITING

I haven't yet met an author who reported that their writing process took them less time than anticipated. If you are such an author, I would love to know your secret. Perhaps you should write a book about how to write a book. As lovely as it would be to sit down and write after having done a bit of planning and outlining, every writer has to deal with certain obstacles to writing. I think it's helpful to be transparent about those obstacles, anticipate them, and call them out before you actually encounter them.

Whenever I start a project or do any kind of long-term planning, I like to start by anticipating the potential obstacles and challenges that I might encounter.* This helps me to feel more grounded and less defeated or caught off guard when inevitable setbacks occur. It also gives me a chance to strategize a bit about what I can do to push

---

* I learned this technique from Tara McMullin (https://www.whatworkspodcast. com/).

through or overcome these obstacles, so I'm never caught off guard or stuck without having some kind of action to take. This is the reason I included Exercise 4 as one of your pre-reading exercises (see the Introduction).

When writing this book, I created a roadmap and included, for example, a list of who is on my support team. I also asked myself questions like:

- Who can I reach out to when I'm feeling stuck?
- Who can be a hype person for me when I start to doubt myself?
- Who is a good accountability partner for me?
- Who do I know who is also working on a book and who might be interested in doing some coworking sessions?
- Who might be willing to read parts of the book and give me honest feedback?

Building a support system is a great way to prepare to overcome obstacles as you write. Collaboration is key (I will continue to beat this drum until the whole world falls in lockstep behind me). There's really no reason to sit in solitude and write your book like a sequestered monk. I can't emphasize enough how much having different brains around who can help you wrangle your own brain is a wonderful thing. So let's consider some common obstacles and how to manage them.

MINDSET CHALLENGES

Speaking of brains, as much as you need your brain to write your book, your brain could be one of the biggest obstacles—if not *the* biggest—to writing you face. It's tricky like that! As a big idea expert,

I'd say it's quite likely that you'll encounter some mindset challenges at some point in the writing process. Mindset challenges like ...

PERFECTIONISM

The Challenge: Nothing can halt progress faster than a perfectionist mindset. When I told you about my previous habit of writing and rewriting philosophy paper outlines, that was my perfectionism going into overdrive and getting the best of me. I was afraid to write a sentence without checking and double-checking it. That made my writing feel very stilted, abrasive, black-and-white, and academic. I admire those who can write complex, impeccably sound logical arguments that are also elegant, memorable, and even humorous. It's one of the hardest writing tasks. I eventually found a philosophical style with more personality, but then my tone wasn't always received as rigorous enough for academic work. My personal writing style lends itself better to business writing, and I've leaned into that strength hard. But I digress. The point is that perfectionism is a big obstacle to writing anything, including business books.

The Solution: One of my favorite techniques for letting go of perfectionism is to treat everything I share publicly as a minimally viable product. You'll see me talking about a minimally viable marketing plan (MVMP) in Part 3, for example. When you treat what you write as the "final word," that's when perfectionism runs amok. If, instead, you can think of everything you write as your "considered view of the moment," it invites a lot of freedom. And it helps to remember that you can always amend what you say. There's absolutely no shame in changing your mind.

Again, your book is a snapshot of your brain. Come back to your book in a year and you'll have a different perspective, no matter how perfect it is. While the fundamentals might not change, you will likely have new insights, experience new contexts, and encounter new examples that would enhance what you've written. In some cases, you may even do a complete 180-degree turn on something you've said, but that can be a great way to frame a conversation with your reader. This is another reason I insist that it's a waste of time to spend years writing a business book. If you treat your book as the final word, you can get caught in an infinite loop of editing and adding to what you said previously—talk about a vicious circle. Instead, write for a sustained period of time (i.e., 80 days) and share the snapshot or minimal viable product.

FEAR

The Challenge: Do not be alarmed if you experience some fear along your journey. I would be more surprised to find that you didn't encounter fear. One of the first business books I read after starting my business in 2015 was Tara Mohr's *Playing Big: Find Your Voice, Your Mission, Your Message*. And the big ideas from that book stick with me to this day. *Playing Big* taught me how to defang my inner critic (I call her "Maude," no offense to sweet Maude played by Ruth Gordon in *Harold and Maude*, which is one of my favorite films). Mohr talks about how fear is a natural response to learning to play big. When we step outside of our comfort zones, fear naturally creeps in as our brain's way of trying to keep us safe. It's a natural defense mechanism, not something to feel ashamed about or try to get rid of. So to expect not to feel any fear when we work to expand our capacity is an unrealistic expectation.

The Solution: Instead of expecting that we won't feel fear in these legitimately scary situations, what we can do is have gratitude for our brain keeping us safe (thanks, Maude!) and tell ourselves that we're going to do the thing anyway. It's all about having a growth mindset instead of letting the fear stop us in our tracks.

Recognize that you will feel fear whenever you do anything new—what Brené Brown calls FFTs (f*cking first times). If writing a book is new to you, then you're going to experience some fear. Often, even the self-awareness that you are feeling fear and that fear is a perfectly normal response to playing big can be enough to overcome this obstacle.

The next question is, What will you do when you experience fear? A lot of people benefit from journaling about their fear. You can, for instance, write a letter to your fear. Do it now when you're feeling relaxed, and do it later when the fear creeps in. It's amazing how much writing to your fear can help you make friends with it.

Not big into journaling? I get it. When you're writing a book, it can be hard to find time or brain space to write recreationally. I almost never pick up my journal when I'm deep into my creative mode. Perhaps your strategy for getting over your fear will be to call a friend and name your fear or do some breathwork. Or maybe you're the type of person who can reframe their fear as motivation. Whatever works for you. Take some time to think about what you'll do to move through your fear.

FEELING LIKE AN IMPOSTER

The Challenge: A close cousin of fear is that imposter feeling. Some refer to it as imposter syndrome, but it's not actually recognized by the DSM, so I prefer to talk about it as a feeling (doesn't make it any less real, by the way). Women and other under-recognized people are especially susceptible to imposter feelings because our culture drills into our brains that we need to "be good," by which they mean not stepping out of bounds or speaking out of turn, if we want to earn our place. And so much of the time, when we are "good," it feels like we're not "good enough" because the gatekeepers won't make space for us at the table no matter what we do. Power dynamics have nothing to do with your worth. We are all enough.

Consequently, whenever we decide to do anything we're worried might be perceived as not staying in our own lanes, like writing a book or cultivating a thought leadership ecosystem, we wonder if we're really worthy to speak on the topic. To be honest, the term "thought leader" makes me cringe whenever I use it (despite using it in my subtitle). I also alluded to this in the Introduction. As a buzzword, "thought leadership" perpetuates the misperception that only certain authority figures are worthy to speak. "Thought leader" also calls to mind privileged, navel-gazing narcissists anointing themselves as "leaders of thought." If you are a true thought leader, then others should recognize that in you. It's not that I think the term shouldn't exist, though; I just bristle at the arrogance required to call yourself a thought leader. This is why I like "big idea expert" better, though I know that many women and under-recognized people have just as much trouble calling themselves "experts" as "thought leaders." I'm on a mission to make the world safe for all big idea experts.

The Solution: The question to ask yourself the next time you experience feelings of being an imposter or feeling like a fraud is, Who gets to decide you're "worthy" to speak? There are no credentials that will magically turn you from an imposter to an authority—except maybe writing your book and proving to yourself that you're not an imposter.

Still, simply standing up to that voice inside your head might not be enough to overcome this obstacle. You also need to take action to prove to your brain that you are worthy to speak. It can help to remember a time when you did overcome your imposter feelings and things turned out even better than you could have imagined. You may want to start keeping a list of all those times—your own "hype" file. Add to your file:

- The big presentation that stretched you and stretched the edges of your comfort zone and turned out even better than you could have imagined
- The time you went for that job or promotion that you thought you might not be ready for and then got it
- That moment of recognition that came at just the right moment
- The boss moves you've made in your business
- The leaps of faith that paid off most handsomely
- The client testimonials that warmed your heart and brought a tear to your eye

WRITER'S BLOCK

The Challenge: Writer's block is one of the best-known obstacles to writing—it's kind of the poster child for writing obstacles. But we give writer's block way too much power. What is it? It is described as some kind of paralyzing feeling that stops the words from coming to our brains. Most of us haven't thought deeper than this feeling. We need to dig deeper to get to the core of our writer's block, though. The truth is I'm a writer's block denier. Let me explain why.

Whenever I drill down on my "writer's block," what I find is that the issue is not merely not knowing what to write. Most often, it's actually fear or imposter syndrome that keeps me from starting to write. Maude inserts herself and tells me that whatever words come to mind are not the right words, and suddenly I'm spiraling into a place of second-guessing every word that comes to mind.

Or I find that it's not writer's block so much as ideator's block. It's not about the writing. It's about the ideas. Perhaps I haven't done enough research to talk about a topic. In more cases, I simply haven't done enough thinking about what I think.

The Solution: In these cases, I remind myself how much thinking happens during the act of writing itself. If I just start, most of the time, the ideas start to flow. So if you're feeling writer's block, the best thing you can do is start writing.

I know it sounds like I'm punking you—"the solution to writer's block is to write"—but I'm not trying to be glib. If you don't know what to write, write absolutely anything you can think of. Just start. This is where it's actually an advantage to be writing a messy first draft of a book. As long as you have an outline, you've got several chapters where you can dip in and write some stuff. Get stuck working on Chapter 1? Hop over to Chapter 5. Get stuck there? No problem, write a section of Chapter 2. There are no rules about writing your book straight through from start to finish. Even if your chapters build on each other, you can still hop back and forth between the more basic, earlier chapters and the later chapters that bring everything together. Structure and order can be fixed in the edit. Never forget.

So the next time you experience writer's block, first, dig down deeper on that feeling. What is it telling you? Do you need to do more research? Do you need some more reflecting time? Beware of any false flags, though. Even if you do need to do more research, you should write whatever you can before you start down any rabbit holes. Even if you do need more reflecting time, there's reflection that's productive and reflection that's a procrastination mechanism. An easy way to tell the difference is to talk to a good friend. Having someone else as a sounding board for your ideas is a great way to get those juices flowing. So take your reflections to the streets and then write down whatever you say (or even better, record your conversation). Then, most important, remind yourself that thinking comes through the act of expressing your thoughts and that you have lots of time to "get it right."

Also, perfectionism, fear, and imposter syndrome often masquerade as writer's block. Messy is exactly where you want to be. Editing is a problem for "future you." Take a cue from Mark Twain, who said, "Writing is easy. All you have to do is cross out the wrong words." Right now, your problem is simply that you don't have all the *right* words you need to finish your book. Start finding those words and refuse to believe in writer's block—like Tinker Bell, writer's block can't exist if you don't believe in it.

OVERWHELM

The Challenge: One final common obstacle to writing is the feeling of overwhelm. As a business owner, there's no doubt you've written countless articles, blog posts, social media posts, pitch decks, proposals, presentations, talks, etc. You've probably written some stuff (maybe even a lot of stuff) on your book topic already. So why do you feel overwhelmed when it comes to writing your book?

Well, simply put, a book is longer. You might also be putting a lot of pressure on yourself because writing a book feels momentous—it feels like the last word on the topic (even though I don't want you to think of it that way). Books feel somehow more permanent than anything we write for the internet. There's that image we have of our book sitting on a shelf in our home or a library for ever and ever, amen. You may also be thinking of your book as your legacy. Even though it's not merely a legacy piece for you, there's still this sense that your book is a way to outrun your own mortality. Your book will live on after you, and what will happen when you're not around to defend yourself?

The Solution: Yeah, all of these thoughts are quite overwhelming. To avoid feeling overwhelmed, focus on the small pieces. Just like running a marathon for the first time will feel overwhelming if you think, "How will I be able to run 26.2 miles?" writing a book will feel overwhelming if you think, "How will I be able to write 40,000+ words?" How would you go about running a marathon for the first time? At the risk of sounding trite, the answer is one step at a time.

Instead of "How will I be able to run 26.2 miles?" you ask yourself, "How will I be able to run one mile?" Approach writing your book in the same way—one chapter, one section, one paragraph, one sentence, one word at a time. If you're feeling overwhelmed, forget about the big picture for a bit (at least long enough to hit your word count goal for the day) and focus on writing something small. It can help to ask yourself my favorite question: "What is the tiniest step I can take toward meeting my goal?"* With running a marathon, that might be putting on your shoes. Here that might be opening your document.

YOU DON'T NEED MY PERMISSION NOT TO WRITE YOUR BOOK

Finally, if these obstacles to writing simply feel like too much, you always have the option not to write your book. I stand by what I said earlier: if you don't have a business case for your book, it's not the highest and best use of your time, and you shouldn't write it. Period. *But* even if you do have a business case for your book, and you do need a book for your business, you don't need to write it yourself. There are other ways to get your book written, which are worth considering.

In case you missed all of my not-so-subtle hints so far, I'm a ghostwriter. I spend a lot of time writing business books for entrepreneurs, experts, and leaders who have more ideas than time to write them down. Many of my clients would love to write their own books if only they didn't have the pesky problem of also having to run their businesses (which usually require more than 40 hours of their time every week). Many of my clients have no desire at all to write their own books. Either way, working with a ghostwriter is nothing to feel ashamed or bad about. There are some things in my business that I outsource that I wish I had time to do myself (e.g., graphic design).

---

* This is also the premise behind James Clear's great book, *Atomic Habits*.

There are many more things in my business that I outsource because I have absolutely no desire to do them (e.g., bookkeeping). I don't face an identity crisis every time I review my monthly transactions sent by my bookkeeper, nor do I worry that asking a graphic designer to design presentation templates or event promo images calls into question my expertise. There's no ethical difference between hiring a bookkeeper or a graphic designer and hiring a ghostwriter (at least, not the way I work with my ghostwriting clients).

I think where people get hung up on the ethical aspect of working with a ghostwriter is where they see ghostwriters "subbing" for the expert themselves. And I agree. This brings back all of the plagiarism nightmares I worried about as a professor. While I'm sure there are some ghostwriters who use their subject matter expertise to write for others who end up being the face of those ideas (think Cyrano de Bergerac writing for his friend Christian to win over Roxane's heart), I'm constitutionally incapable of operating this way. Sure, ChatGPT and I could write the first draft of your book without even talking to you, but would that book sound like you? Would that book add any value above what your reader could find by googling, reading Wikipedia, or playing around with ChatGPT themselves? The value that comes from working with a ghostwriter is in the collaborative aspect. Not only am I your ghostwriter, I'm your thought partner—talk about a solution to writer's block. When it works well, a beautiful mind meld happens, and the book that's produced is something better than either my client or I could write alone. So if your writing obstacles start to pile up, consider whether working with a ghostwriter could be your complete solution.

As long as you can find someone who will collaborate with you using your ideas, outsourcing the writing will get you to a full manuscript, certainly faster and perhaps with a better result. Wouldn't you be proud to share a book that sounds like you on your very best writing day? You have to ask yourself why it should matter how that book gets written.

Chapter 5

THE IDEATION PROCESS

Because you are putting your big idea in the driver's seat, the most important thing you can do for your book during the planning phase is to find an ideation process that works for you. When I work with my ghostwriting clients on idea development, we start with the premise that no idea is off limits.

First, we let 100 flowers bloom,* and then we prune our bouquet. In the early stages, the last thing you want to do is dismiss an idea. If it comes up in your mind, it's worth considering even if you quickly decide it doesn't belong here. Freeing your mind is necessary to get to the real nuggets of content gold you're trying to find.

---

* A classic quote from Mao Zedong. Here I would like to invoke the spirit of Kelly Diels's (https://kellydiels.com/) standard email disclaimer: "Just 'cuz I mention someone's work does not mean we know each other. It doesn't mean they even know I exist nor does it mean that they like me or approve of my work. Nor does it mean I endorse them unequivocally or that they endorse me. It means that there's a particular cultural thing that I'm trying to talk about and an idea or project of their's is relevant and I want to give credit where credit is due [sic]."

MIND MAPPING

There are several ways to begin the ideation process for your business book. I recommend starting the ideation process with some mind mapping sessions. Even if you've never tried mind mapping (I never used this method to write philosophy papers; I discovered it only after I started my business, though I now wonder how it would have worked for me in that capacity), some version will work for you—you simply need to experiment until you find what works.

Earlier, I said to think of yourself as painting with words. In other words, you want to create your business book like a painter creates a portrait. Like a sketch artist, you need to have a rough sketch of your book before you start writing. This is where mind mapping comes in.

I first used this method when I wanted to create an online course for DIY authors. Here are the steps I followed:

STEP 1: RAPID IDEATION

I grabbed a stack of note cards and furiously wrote down every topic idea I could think of about writing a business book. I ignored the urge to edit my ideas at this stage.

STEP 2: GROUPING LIKE IDEAS

Then I took my stack of topic ideas and grouped them into rough categories.

STEP 3: TAKING OUT THE TRASH

Then I decided what belonged and what didn't. I looked for ideas that might belong in a different course or be too far afield for what I wanted to teach.

STEP 4: ARRANGING IDEAS INTO MODULES

From here, I took the remaining ideas and put them in an order that made sense. As I played with these ideas, the modules and lessons within began to emerge. This is the magic of mind mapping!

STEP 5: LET IT SIMMER

I did steps 1–4 in a single sitting, leaving my note cards sitting out on the rug (I like to do creative work like this on the floor. If you have little ones or pets running around the house, you will probably want to use a table or some other, less-trafficked area in your home). After getting to this point, I slept on it.

STEP 6: WHAT'S MISSING?

When I came back to my mind map with a fresh head, I asked if there were any modules or lessons that were missing and filled in any gaps.

STEP 7: MINIMUM VIABLE PRODUCT (MVP)

Once the process felt complete and I was satisfied with my result, I had the outline of my course. I wrote out the list of modules and lessons, and I was ready to start creating my script and slides.

You can follow a similar process with your book. Besides the note card method described above, I have also been known to grab a huge piece of butcher paper, lay it out on the floor, and go to town writing down words and connecting them into a big web of ideas. A notebook, sticky notes, or a whiteboard are also fine tools for mind mapping. If you prefer digital to analog, there are a lot of great mind mapping apps available. I like playing with Miro, for example.

Choosing exactly how you use this method is less important than diving in and getting your ideas out. You may need to try a few different methods before you find what works for you.

I find that doing three to five mind mapping sessions, possibly using different methods, over the course of a few days or a week helps me to find the kernel of an idea that I can cultivate into a topic idea. This is a good place to start, especially if outlining feels too linear to you.

INSPIRING YOURSELF AND GATHERING CONTENT

This next part is my favorite part of the planning stage, and sadly, it's one that a lot of first-time authors skip altogether. Once you have the rough sketch of what you're going to write about, it's time to do some treasure hunting. This is your chance to mine your own content, looking for gold nuggets of ideas that you want to include in your book. I talk about this process as inspiring yourself and gathering content to repurpose. While you may stumble upon some words that you can cut and paste directly, in most cases you'll find a flash of an idea that spurs you to write something new or to connect some dots. The goal is repurposing your content, not necessarily recycling.

If you haven't already, now is the time to start a folder on your computer—a cozy little place where your business book will hang out in its embryonic state. Next, look through all of your blog articles, social media posts, online course modules, presentation notes, and any relevant content you've created and drop those files into your folder. As you find ideas that you want to include in your book, make notes to yourself about why you think each one should be included. The more specific you can be in your notes to yourself, the easier it will be to incorporate them into your messy draft later. Take your time with this. It could be a fun activity to do on a quiet morning or afternoon.

Case studies in particular are content gold mines, especially if you're writing a how-to book. Not only will you find information you can use about your process and the results you provide, but you'll also find words from your clients' perspective, which will give you an idea of what others find most valuable about what you do. These are key clues for positioning and promoting your book.

Now, I've intentionally suggested sifting through your content *after* you've mapped out your idea. There's a good reason for this. While I have worked with authors who start by gathering content—they have several blog articles that they would like to turn into a book, for example—I find this process very difficult. Every piece of content you create lives within a specific context. It can be very difficult to extract a piece of content from that context and drop it in the middle of a totally different context (see: your book being a snapshot of your brain at a certain point in time). I have been writing monthly blog articles for my business for the past eight years. I can't imagine gathering up all 177 of those blog articles and trying to find a common thread running throughout all of those pieces. That would be an utter disaster. While it may be true that the idea for this book has been percolating since I started my business, my business and my mindset have changed too much for that to work. Still, the odds are good you've built your way to the idea that is your book idea, so some of what you wrote two years ago or even eight years ago will be relevant.

Rather than gathering your previous content and hoping to stumble on your big idea hiding in there, a better process is to intentionally let your big idea come to you first and then look at your older content through the lens of that idea. Take an honest look at what you have, and don't spare the sword. It's easier to carve out a new piece of content than to try to smash an ill-fitting piece into the puzzle. This is the way to honor that symbiotic relationship between your idea and yourself.

One more word of caution here: beware of getting lost in the research. Recall that the big trap to avoid at this stage is doing too much planning. You might not believe me, but it is possible to do too much planning, and it is possible to do too much research (including researching your own content). Keep in mind that your goal here is to find the gold in your previous writing and weave that into the fine tapestry you've already started. Avoid gathering content as a procrastination mechanism. Get in and get out so you can get to the writing stage.

VALIDATING YOUR IDEA

In case you're getting the message that I want you to be hasty—with all this talk about not doing too much planning, writing quickly, thinking of your book as a snapshot of your brain, and getting in and getting out—I want you to know that rushing through is not at all the goal. Life's too short to write a sh*tty book, and there's too much sh*tty content available already (and more is written every day by humans and robots). This is why I absolutely want you to validate your idea before you start writing.

There are a number of ways to do this as well. And this is also a place where you'll want to exercise caution, because if you ask too many people (or the wrong people) in an effort to validate your idea, you may end up watering down your idea or changing it into something you don't actually want to write. So beware of who you're asking, and make sure you feel strongly enough about your idea to defend it when the criticisms show up (because they will).

I encourage you to talk about your book early and often. Sharing half-baked ideas is scary, but it is the only way to get the feedback you need in the early stages to make your book exceptional. Remember, criticism is what you want at this stage. You are looking for the feedback that will help you hone your idea. But you also want to feel some conviction. The time to validate your idea is when you feel finished "fishing" for ideas, and you have some confidence that you know what your book is about. You're looking for validation that you're heading in the right direction or criticism that turns you away from a bad idea. It is possible that you'll decide you're heading in the totally wrong direction, and that's okay. It's better to find that out at this stage, when you haven't sunk a lot of time and effort into the idea. You can always change course and start over with mind mapping. Please make sure that this is your decision, though, not someone forcing something on you. I know plenty of marketing experts who have wanted to steer my content in a particular direction over the years. I took a lot of their advice (which sometimes paid off), but ultimately, I had to stay true to my own expertise as well and remind myself that at the end of the day, smashing book marketing and sales records is not my end goal. Hold on to your idea loosely at this stage, but do hold on to it. Make your mind up before you start sharing so that it will take a convincing argument before you'll let it go.

VALIDATION METHODS

As far as validation methods go, one easy way to get feedback is to do some simple market research. Come up with a list of people you want to talk to about your idea and set meetings with them. They should be part of your target audience or people who work closely with your target audience. Talk to everyone on your list individually, and only talk to them about the parts of the book where you believe they could be most helpful. You could also do an informal focus group and meet with several people at once.

Another good place to share your book idea and get feedback in real time is on LinkedIn. In fact, LinkedIn is a fabulous place to build an audience of people who could buy the book. It's also a great testing ground for big ideas, so while you're writing the book, don't be afraid to make LinkedIn your personal idea incubator. It's the perfect place to float half-baked ideas. Who knows? The conversation you start could lead you to your best ideas yet.

Here's how I recommend using LinkedIn to validate your business book idea:

- Share your book's most innovative and controversial ideas in bite-size chunks and see how people react.
- Not only does this help you validate your ideas, but also it jump-starts your marketing and gives you some accountability if you choose to share that you're writing a book, which isn't necessary, by the way. If you're not yet ready to share that part, you can easily share nuggets of ideas from your book without announcing what you are doing with those nuggets.
- Don't be afraid to share less than fully worked out ideas. Sharing on social media should feel more low-stakes. Here's why: if you discover in this process that an idea shouldn't see the light of day, you can drop it before you spend a lot of time chasing it down or feeling the embarrassment of publishing it and getting that criticism later.

Whatever you do, though, don't skip the validation step. Having affirmation that you're on the right track will be a huge motivator as you march forward into the writing process. So let's get into it!

Part 2

WRITING YOUR WAY ACROSS THE FINISH LINE

At this point, you've done enough planning to get down to business—the business of writing your business book. You might not feel ready, though. You might be convinced that you need to read some books about writing (besides this one), for example, but reading half a dozen books on writing is almost certainly a distraction that you don't need. What do you expect to accomplish by reading books on writing? Be honest.

Maybe you think you need to "brush up" on grammar and the mechanics of writing. If you're like most of my clients, though, you've taken plenty of English classes, and your understanding of the mechanics of writing is good enough. Besides, fixing the technical stuff is a job for a good editor (more on this later).

Despite what you may be thinking, writing a book is not that different from writing a social media post or a blog article. Sure, the style and tone may be different. Writing for analog is different from writing for digital because we read differently when holding a physical book in our hands vs. reading on a screen. You also can't simply string together several blog articles or LinkedIn posts and call it a book (I mean, you *can*, but that's not what I would recommend). These are important considerations. But what you need the most is an idea that's big enough to sustain a book's worth of content. And you won't find out whether your idea fits the bill with your nose buried in other books or contemplating all the boxes you need to check with your book.

The only way to discover if you have a business book in you is by getting down to business. It's something for you to discover as you write, not something you'll figure out by spending a ton of time overthinking the how, where, and when. You will learn the most from letting your fingers slide along the keyboard and following your intuition. And even if your book does have some mechanical issues, you (or your editor) will easily be able to fix them later.

Another thing you might be thinking now is that you need to read all of your competitors' books. You might believe that in order to position your book as unique compared to all the other books in the same category, you need to read at least the top ten books. Here's why that's a bad idea:

- It could backfire. You may end up reading a book that you think is too similar to what you're planning to write, and it could make you second guess your idea.

- It could lead to (unintentional) plagiarism. No matter how carefully you take notes and do your own research, if you read too many books on your topic, it can become hard to disentangle your ideas from those of others. You could end up polluting your thoughts, filling your head with irrelevant information that will distract you, and ultimately making your writing job harder.
- It can become a procrastination mechanism. Perhaps you decide to restrict yourself to reading only the top three books in your book's category. Well, each of those books will likely reference other books. You'll feel you need to read those as well (or at least "dip into them") and so on *ad infinitum*. It's a vicious circle.

I'm not suggesting that you shouldn't read books on writing or check out your competition, not at all. What I'm suggesting is that you wait to do this work until *after* you've gotten the bulk of your draft finished. Once you have a full draft of your book, feel free to read as many books on writing and as many other of your competitors' business books as your heart desires. For now, the number-one thing you can do is start getting words down onto the page as quickly as possible. Above all, this means not overthinking it.

TRAP #2: OVERTHINKING THE WRITING

Earlier I said that one way to sum up all three of the traps I talk about in this book is the mistake of overthinking the writing and underthinking everything else. As a chronic overthinker, I've had to train myself to recognize when I'm overthinking and to immediately take action. Even taking the smallest action I can think of in the moment will snap me out of my rumination. This is a good skill to have when you're writing a book.

Many big idea experts get stuck because of overthinking. You may be writing along and then, all of a sudden, you start questioning yourself. Maybe you think of a statistic that you want to include in your book, for example, and you want to look up the exact number. So you google it, and 30 minutes later, you haven't been able to put your finger on the exact statistic you want, though you may have found all kinds of interesting data points, some relevant to your topic, others not so much (not to mention 21 recipes for 30-minute weeknight meals, a new Substack you want to subscribe to, and a great pair of sandals for your upcoming beach vacation). You feel frustrated. You're kicking yourself for falling down an internet rabbit hole. Then you start questioning the point you're trying to make and maybe your whole book. Before you know it, you're spiraling out of control.

Whenever you find yourself falling into an overthinking spiral like this, I want you to stop and go back to writing—preferably before you get to the point of questioning your whole book. Write what you know. Leave a note to yourself about the statistic or the research and move on. You can fix it in the edit. To avoid this kind of shame spiral, whenever possible, I recommend doing the research *after* you have a complete rough draft. It's easier to make a call about a particular statistic or piece of research when you can see the big picture, and research done after content creation is a very different animal from research done while you're in the throes of getting your idea down on the page. All of this will help you avoid overthinking.

Of course, if you're writing a very research-intensive kind of book, then it may be impossible to wait until you have a rough draft before doing your research. If this is the case, I have two suggestions:

- Consider whether this is the best type of business book for you to write. You could be writing a reference book for experts in your industry, in which case a research-intensive book might be exactly what you should write. If you're writing for a lay audience, however, you may want to rethink how much research you're sharing.
- Gather all of your research together at the beginning so that you can simply write. Or try gathering the research you need for one chapter, then write that chapter before moving onto the next chapter. I find that I get into trouble whenever I try to research and write at the same time. So do whatever you can to create that separation.

Another thing that helps you avoid overthinking is reminding yourself that your business book is not a credential. Yes, there are good reasons for you to write your book: you have a business case for your book; you've established your book's "why." But publishing your book doesn't make you an expert. You're already an expert; your expertise is simply unwritten. As you start putting words on the page, do your best to stay away from overthinking, at least until you finish your messy first draft. You can fix it all in the edit.

The goal of Part 2 is to show you how to get to your messy first draft as quickly as possible. This way you'll preserve your energy for positioning, publishing, and promoting (Part 3).

Chapter 6

TRANSLATE YOUR BUSINESS IDEA INTO A BOOK IDEA

When I talk about the work I do with my ghostwriting clients, I often call myself a translator of ideas. The best clients are subject matter experts who are happy to share and ramble on (I mean this in the most loving way possible) about their ideas with my team and me. Our job is to turn subject matter experts into big idea experts. We do this by gaining a lay understanding of their topic, both from the inside out and from the outside in, so that we can translate those ideas for their audience.

You've probably had the experience of talking to an expert outside of your own industry or discipline and feeling like they were speaking a different language—I often have this experience when talking to a techy person about tech problems, for instance. It takes a special leader or expert who can write or talk in a way that makes sense to nonleaders and nonexperts. When you spend most of your time interacting with other subject matter experts, it's easy to create an echo chamber.

This is where being a business owner can be an advantage. You likely don't spend all of your time in an echo chamber. Still, as an author, you'll need to be aware of the times when you need to break out of that echo chamber and translate your idea. Are you using jargon that you need to explain? Have you spelled out all of the acronyms that may leave your readers scratching their heads? There are few things more annoying as a reader than seeing an acronym and not knowing what it stands for. In a physical book, it might be easy enough for me to flip back to the introduction or the beginning of the chapter and find the answer, but if I'm reading on my Kindle (or listening to an audiobook), then all bets are off. I might google it. Or I might just keep going and hope that I'll be able to make sense of what I'm reading from the context.

Avoid giving your reader a headache by spelling out acronyms or avoiding them where they aren't crucial to the transformation you want your reader to make. This way they'll stay focused on what you want them to be thinking instead of playing alphabet guessing games. With this in mind, let's consider what it means to translate your business book idea for your audience.

IT'S NOT "DUMBING DOWN"

First, let's look at what translating your idea does not mean. If you worry that translating your work for your readers means dumbing yourself down, I have two questions for you: (a) So what? And (b) Do you feel as if you're dumbing down your content every time you explain what you do to a nonexpert?

If you worry that in writing your book, you're dumbing down your content, explore what you mean by "dumbing down" and what about that makes you bristle. There's some underlying fear. What is the fear that comes up for you here? Are you worried that other experts in your field will judge you for being overly simplistic or "selling out?" If so, then you need to consider who your audience is. Go back to your book's why and reflect on that in relation to the alleged "dumbing down" of your expertise. Perhaps what you'll find is that you're naturally using simpler language because it's more compatible with the transformation you want to lead your nonexpert reader through. Most business books are written for nonexperts, so that a book is simple and easy to understand is probably a plus.

Perhaps the fear that you're dumbing down your work comes not from a fear of what other experts will think but from a past criticism you received in school or from a superior at work. Again, these worries will likely disappear if you focus on connecting with your audience. For example, the content of this book would be very different if I were writing a book about writing for other ghostwriters. Would a ghostwriter find this book overly simplistic and surface-level? Possibly, but I'm not writing it for them, so why should I worry about that? To connect with an expert, you speak differently than when you connect with a nonexpert. If you try to write your book in the same way you'd write a presentation to give at your annual professional conference, then you won't connect with your audience. However, when you can explain your work so simply that a nonexpert could learn how to do it, then not only will they start to think of you as the go-to expert, but they will also be able to talk about your book with their friends. If this is "dumbing down" your work, then I say let's get dumber. There's a reason that the series of books "for dummies" with the yellow cover sold millions of copies.

However, if your concern is that you're dumbing down your ideas too much *for your audience*, then that's something to look at more closely. When I'm talking about translating your ideas, I am thinking of something very different from dumbing down your ideas. Primarily, I'm thinking about how to connect with your audience, and that's where I want your focus as well. That's what I want you to consider when you think about translating your idea for your people.

DIFFERENCES BETWEEN READERS AND ONE-ON-ONE CLIENTS

Besides making sure that you are writing at a level that will connect with your readers, you will also want to be aware of how a reader might use the content you're sharing vs. how your client might use the content you're sharing. Even if you are picturing your reader as one of your clients (something I definitely recommend), there are certain limitations that you face in writing a book. When you work with your clients, you can tailor your recommendations based on their specific needs. For instance, you can recommend a solution and then check in on the results before recommending a different solution. You likely won't be able to do the same thing in the same way for your readers.

Consider how you might navigate this difference as you write your messy first draft. Perhaps you need to add some exercises for readers to help them diagnose their own problem, which you might not need to share with clients, for example. When I edited a book for a leadership coach, we had to conquer this challenge. She realized that when she works one-on-one with her clients, she meets with them weekly and could give them different exercises based on what was going on in their professional and personal lives as well as what past exercises had been most effective. Obviously, she couldn't do the same for her readers. But she could share a menu of possible practices in the book, add a section helping her readers decide which of the 16 different exercises might be most helpful for them, and explain how to do each practice. She recommended that they spend one week doing one of the exercises every day before moving on to try the next. Then, once they discovered which exercises resonated with them the most, they could concentrate on those and reach out to her for additional exercises or recommendations, of course.

So as you write, consider how you might guide your readers in a way that's different from how you might guide a client or someone you're working with one-on-one. You want to give readers a flavor of what it's like to work with you, but you also want your readers to experience a transformation. And it's important to remember that your reader's transformation might be different from what your one-on-one clients experience, and that's okay.

Chapter 7

THE MESSY FIRST DRAFT

O kay, having read the previous section as a bit of warm-up; take a deep breath now. You have made it to the point where you're ready to start writing. Yep. It's that time.

Up until this point, you've been planning, mind mapping, gathering content, ideating, and validating. You should have a pretty clear picture of what your book will look like by now. If you don't feel clear, revisit the pre-reading exercises in the introduction as well as past chapters to make sure that you feel comfortable with your big idea. I really want you to feel excited about your idea and the readers who will be transformed by reading your business book before you continue. If you don't feel any excitement, that's something to examine too. It's easy to believe before you start writing that you will be able to power through on an idea that isn't all that exciting (I've been there). But even if this were true, why not find a big idea that's both valuable for your readers and satisfying for you to write? There are millions of ideas; choose wisely.

This is important: if you're feeling lackluster at this point, it will be tough for you to take your book across the finish line, let alone enthusiastically market your book. And it's simply not worth your time to write a book (or more likely, half or three-quarters of a book) if you feel like you're simply going through the motions. You're a business owner. Your time is precious. Above all, you need to be convinced that writing your book is the highest and best use of your time, because it's taking time away from other revenue-generating tasks. So only move forward if you can't imagine not writing this book.

Now that that's out of the way, let's get to the how-to of writing your messy first draft.*

OUTLINING

First, it should be acknowledged that there are many ways to get a book manuscript written. I don't intend for anything I say in the rest of this chapter to serve as prescriptive; the writing process that's best for you is the one that works for you. What I share here is not so much best practices as a bucket of tips and ideas that have worked for me and others. Outlining is the first of these.

Because many find the outlining process to be overly linear and have a hard time diving straight from topic idea into an outline, I recommend starting with the mind mapping process I walked you through in Chapter 5. If you did the mind mapping as I recommended, you have a pile of note cards, a notebook full of your chicken scratch, a piece of butcher paper or a whiteboard splashed with a web of ideas, or a digital map of your big idea hanging out somewhere on your

---

* Anne Lamott famously introduces the concept of "Sh*tty First Drafts" in her excellent book *Bird by Bird*. The biggest difference between Lamott's SFD and my MFD is that she tells herself she never has to share her SFD with anyone and I want you to get comfortable with the idea of sharing your half-baked ideas.

computer. And you might be tempted to go from the mind map straight into drafting. The outlining step is a critical bridge between the non-linear ideation process and the more linear book, though. If you've done the mind mapping, then outlining should feel relatively easy too. Keep in mind that your outline can be very high-level. It can be as minimalist as a list of possible chapters with bullet points under each one. By the way, this is the point where I move from analog to digital, kicking off the writing stage.

To start outlining, open up your favorite word-processing software (I use Google Docs) and imagine how you would teach your book idea. Suppose you have one semester, roughly 12 weeks, to teach everything you want to include in your book. What would you call your course? This can get you started thinking about title ideas. Toss any title ideas you have at the top of your outline or in a separate manuscript document. Titles generally come to me when I'm not thinking about them. So I simply take note of the ideas whenever they show up.

Next, how would you break your course down into lessons or modules? You might decide to break the semester down into three four-week blocks—these are the parts of your book. From there, you can think of each week as a chapter or two. What chapters naturally fit into each of the parts?

Your outline should include parts and chapters. You can get even more fine-grained if you want, dividing each chapter into sections, but going any deeper will land you in overthinking territory. The point is to get to a complete outline to guide your first draft, not spend a lot of time refining your outline.

Going back to Chapter 3, take the sketch you have of your book idea and ask yourself what type of book is the best vehicle for presenting your big idea. Are you writing a how-to book? Then you will probably want a part about preparing to do the process, a part about doing the process, and a part about results to expect or perhaps troubleshooting.

Are you writing an interview book? Then you will start with your guiding theme, which is also the theme to look for when you conduct the expert interviews, and think about how to package that theme into parts. Maybe you'll want to explain why the theme matters in the first part, break down the key elements of the theme in part two, and talk about how the theme applies to different industries or situations in the third part. Of course, you'll include quotes and stories from your interviews throughout the whole book.

Are you writing a business memoir? It probably doesn't make sense to simply write your story in chronological order. Instead, you'll want to identify the business lessons learned and think about which personal stories connect to which lessons. Then you'll want to consider whether those lessons can be categorized and grouped into parts.

Your book doesn't need to have three parts, of course (you may want 10 or 12 chapters without any parts). But I find that three parts is a good place to start. From here, you can start breaking down each part into chapters. There's also no magic number of chapters, and each part doesn't have to have the same number of chapters either. Coming up with an outline should feel pretty natural, so let the ideas flow. If you feel stuck on a particular part, just start adding chapters that you know you want to include. You can always play around with chapter order later. Remember, too, that you can always add new chapters later. The outline you're creating here is a working outline. There is room for additions and subtractions. Don't overthink your outline; it's a tool to help you get started with the writing.

HOW TO SET YOUR WORD COUNT GOAL

As I mentioned in the introduction, I resisted writing a book about how to write a business book for a long time, mainly because I don't have a lot to say about how to write. This is an odd thing for a professional writer to say, I know. Let me explain: my PhD is in philosophy, not writing, and I was mostly a C-student in my English classes throughout college. (I usually managed to pull out a B by the end of the semester, but that was often due to the generosity—or pity?—of my professors, who saw my little type A brain about to explode.) In other words, I don't believe I have a lot of wisdom to impart about writing, and certainly not about the mechanics of writing. I treat writing purely as a practical tool for distributing ideas. No doubt, this helps me avoid overthinking my writing. My philosophy here is that as long as the ideas are great and the writing is good enough, you have done your job.

My superpower, though, is writing quickly. Because I believe this is one of the most valuable skills a ghostwriter can have, I have worked to cultivate this skill. And as you know, I believe writing quickly is the best way for anyone to write a business book too. So while I might not have a lot to share about how to write or how to write well, I can share my method for writing quickly. Still, it's not rocket science; the key is setting a word count goal and hitting that goal.

Once you have your outline, you are ready to do some simple math. It's really simple; I promise. People often ask me how long their book should be. The answer is that it depends. If you're writing a quick and dirty e-book that you want to save as a PDF and sell on your website for $3, then 20,000 words is fine. If you're a great writer, your topic is sufficiently complicated, and your audience wants something like a reference book, you could easily find yourself topping out at 60,000 words or more. (I'm in the process now of finishing a textbook for a client that's over 90,000 words.)

I generally recommend aiming for 40,000 words for your business book. When printed, 40,000 words is about 100–150 pages depending on the dimensions of the book, spacing, margins, and how many images, graphics, or diagrams you include. This is what some people call an "airplane book" (as I mentioned before) because someone could pick it up and read it on a three- or four-hour flight.

Business book readers like to be able to digest a business book on a plane on the way to a conference, in a single afternoon, or over a couple of days on the weekend. The point is not for your audience to spend hours, weeks, and months poring over your tome and being blown away by the artistry of it. Regardless of what type of business book you're writing, the point is for your readers to learn some lessons, do some exercises, and most important, apply what they have learned in their own businesses to see a transformation or realize that they should hire you to help them with that part. This is what makes the experience of writing a business book as a business owner worth the time, effort, and resources you're putting into it.

NOW IT'S TIME FOR YOU TO SET YOUR WORD COUNT GOAL

And yes, I do recommend that you set a word count goal. While some authors prefer to set a time goal (e.g., "I will write for one hour every day"), I find that a time goal won't keep me honest. Spending an hour on my book might mean writing a couple of sentences, then staring off into space, thinking, or making notes or doing some research. This technique has never worked to get me to my messy first draft. I can easily spend an hour *not* doing any writing, and even if I am truly writing for one hour, I find a word count goal is more motivating.

I set my word count goal by doing some simple math. I take my total target word count of 40,000 and divide that by the number of weeks I have until I'd like to have a complete draft. When I work with my ghostwriting clients, for example, it's a 16-week process to write their business books. Ideally, I'll spend the first half, eight weeks, writing a complete rough draft. This means I need to write 5,000 words per week (40,000 / 8 = 5,000 words per week)—see, I told you the math is simple.

Maybe you're going to give yourself six months to write your book. That means you have 24 weeks to work with. If you want to get your full draft done by the midpoint, then you have 12 weeks to finish your messy first draft. That means you only need to write 3,334 words per week (40,000 / 12 = 3,333.33, which I rounded up).

Earlier I said you could write your book in 80 days, consecutively or not, by writing 500 words each time you sit down to write. Whatever time period works for you is fine, but use those numbers to come up with your weekly word count goal.

1.	Write 500 words per day for 80 consecutive days	500 x 80 = 40,000 500 x 7 = 3,500 words per week 40,000 / 3,500 = 11.43 weeks
2.	Write 500 words per day, 5 days per week, for 16 weeks	500 x 80 = 40,000 500 x 5 = 2,500 words per week 40,000 / 2,500 = 16 weeks

You can also come up with a daily word count by dividing your weekly word count by the number of days you plan to write. Personally, I prefer the flexibility of a weekly word count over having a daily word count. Because I like to binge write, I might write 5,000 words in five days or even three days, depending on what my week looks like. As long as I have a few days with big chunks of time set aside for writing, I'm in good shape. It's hard for me to stick to a daily writing routine while also running my business, though.

Now, if you prefer to write in smaller bursts, or if all you have available is 30 minutes between meetings, then a smaller daily word count goal might make more sense for you. If you do choose this route, take James Clear's advice in *Atomic Habits*: if you break your streak (e.g., miss one day of writing), that's okay; just don't let yourself miss two days in a row. This will make it easier to get back on track and resume your streak. Also, keeping your streak going is less important than building a regular writing habit to capture the snapshot of your brain I keep talking about. Steady work over a few months is my recommendation.

Also, don't be afraid to experiment in the beginning. If this is the first time you've attempted writing a book, you may have no idea how long it will take you to reach a set word count goal. For me, I know that I can comfortably write about 500 words an hour. So I need ten hours each week (or 2 hours 5x per week) to reach my 5,000 words. You may be able to write only 250 words in an hour, however. Try doing some timed writing sessions to figure out what feels comfortable to you, then adjust your goal as necessary. You don't need to be a speed writer to get your book done. I promise. You simply need to have a realistic idea of how much you can write in a specific amount of time so you can do the simple math to set your word count goal and then stick with it. The key to setting accurate word count numbers is to notice that this doesn't include time to research, gather content, or interview people. You need to time yourself when you're writing.

EXERCISE: SET YOUR WORD COUNT GOAL

With all of this in mind, sit down and do your simple math. Choose your manuscript deadline (the date when you want to hand your manuscript over to your publisher or have a polished draft ready to self-publish) and reverse engineer using the above suggestions (total word count / number of weeks to full messy draft, which should be half the total number of weeks until your deadline).

Hitting your word count goal, however you decide to break it down, is the surest and quickest way to get to a full draft, albeit messy. And once that draft is finished, you will feel like a million bucks. So make getting your draft done as quickly as possible your top priority during the writing phase. Remember that you can fix anything in the edit (I know I keep saying it), and relatively speaking, editing is the fun part. It will be tempting, but don't indulge in the urge to edit yourself as you write. That's the surest and quickest way to spend years not finishing your first draft.

YOUR BOOK'S TIMELINE

In this section, I want to lay out an example of a book's timeline—this book's timeline. I am sharing this not necessarily so that you can compare your timeline to mine, but to give you an idea of what to expect. It is possible to write a business book in 80 days (or many fewer if you're so inclined), but that may not be realistic if you are also running your business 40-plus hours per week. I chose to publish my book with a hybrid publisher. The type of publisher you choose, as well as other factors such as the physical specs of your book, the type of printing, and where the book will be sold will all affect your book's production timeline. So above all, I want you to set reasonable expectations about what you can do and then be gentle with yourself if and when you deviate from your anticipated timeline.

Also, as you read this section, keep in mind that every book's timeline will look a little different. A number of variables come into play, including your own writing habits, the type of book you're writing, how much research you need to do, and how much time running your business allows you to spend writing your book. For example:

- Do you want to try for a traditional publisher, in which case you'll need to find an agent first?
- Do you need to write a book proposal? If you are going the traditional route, a book proposal is a must, and some hybrid publishers also ask for a book proposal.

- Will you be self-publishing and need to collect freelancers to help with various elements (e.g., book cover design, editing, formatting)?

It's likely that if you try to set up a strict timeline for yourself, things will take longer than you expect, and your timeline will be very different in practice from what it looked like in theory. Anticipate this so that you don't become overly discouraged when you need to adjust your timeline or different parts of the process take longer than expected. That's all part of the journey.

MY BOOK'S TIMELINE

1. January 1, 2023 – I had the thought that I wanted to write a book. (I've had this same thought every January 1 for the past three or four years. I've started and stopped writing this book or variations on this book for the past four years. I created a now-defunct online course called Business Book 90 in 2019, and that was the seed of the idea that I'm bringing to life here.)
2. March 6, 2023 – I joined Brainstorm Road; the idea is to "practice" every day (i.e., spend at least ten minutes on your project each day and ship something each week) for six months and to ship a finished project at the end.*
3. March 15, 2023 – I started participating in Brainstorm Road with gusto (my first idea was to spend six months coming up with a book idea).

---

* https://www.brainstormroad.com

4. March 17, 2023 – I had a conversation with my friend Jill, who reminded me that I already had a book idea and talked me out of spending six months coming up with an idea.

5. March 28–April 2, 2023 – I did my mind mapping and wrote my book outline.

6. April 3–May 1, 2023 – I wrote a book summary (I had set out to write 10,000 words [500 words per chapter]—and I ended up writing more than 20,000 words, which is about halfway to my complete draft).

7. May 2–May 22, 2023 – I continued expanding on my book summary until I had more than 30,000 words.

8. May 22–May 25, 2023 – I went on a book writing retreat with Jill (we escaped to the beach to work on our books for a few days). We each wrote 10,000 words. At the end of the retreat, I had a complete messy draft at more than 40,000 words.

9. June 1–June 30, 2023 – Editing + working on my marketing plan + reading other similar books to clarify positioning + writing the acknowledgements and dedication sections + brainstorming book cover ideas.

10. July 17–July 20, 2023 – I went to Pittsburgh for another writing retreat with Emily and Ravit. I read through my whole draft manuscript and made notes about the edits I wanted to make.

11. July 21–August 21, 2023 – I spoke to other business book authors I knew and asked for recommendations from other book publishing and marketing experts. Questions I asked: Should I hire a developmental editor? Should I try to find an agent and go the traditional publishing route? Do I need someone to help me with

formatting? If I decide to work with a hybrid publisher, what should I expect? What is my budget? I continued to work on my marketing plan.

12. August 23, 2023 – The final ship date for Brainstorm Road. Because I had finished a draft of my book in May, I had technically shipped way ahead of schedule.

13. August 24–October 24, 2023 – I decided against finding an agent and trying for a traditional publisher. I started interviewing hybrid publishers. I crunched the numbers on my publishing budget.

14. October 25, 2023 – I signed a book publishing contract with Amplify Publishing Group, which included a book marketing strategy.

15. October 26–November 19, 2023 – I finished editing my book.

16. November 20, 2023 – I delivered my complete manuscript to the publisher.

17. November 21–December 15, 2023 – The manuscript was out for copy editing while I worked on supplemental marketing materials (e.g., my bio, book description). The copy edits came back, and I accepted or rejected each suggested change.

18. January 1–March 21, 2024 – Designers worked on layout, formatting, cover design, interior design.

19. March 21, 2024–April 29,2024 – I received the final PDF in hand for a final read-through and proof. Amplify staff also did a final proof.

20. April 30, 2024 – The manuscript went to the printer, and we nailed down the release date and an estimated

ship date (about five months after the proofs are approved).

21. April 2024 – I began implementing the marketing strategy.

22. June 2024 – This is the "book-in-hand" date. The physical copies of the book arrived in the warehouse for distribution, and I got to hold my book in my hands for the first time.

23. October 2024 – The book is officially released. This is also the book's publication date and the date when the retailer listing switches from "Preorder" to "In stock/ Available."

DO YOU NEED A FOREWORD?

You have probably noticed that many of the books you read have a foreword. A foreword is like a long book review and is often written by someone whom readers respect (e.g., an expert in the field, one of the author's mentors). It can give the book a status boost. This endorsement comes at the beginning of the book and often puts the book in context or tells readers why it's important that this book was written at this particular time in history.

You may be wondering whether your book needs a foreword. There are a few reasons you may want to get someone to write a foreword for you. Having a foreword signals to your readers that they have picked up a book that other experts "in the know" are willing to put their stamp of approval on. So having a foreword can give your book some added clout. Instead of simply writing a book and slapping it up on Amazon, taking the extra step of getting someone with some name recognition to write a foreword shows that you have put some additional effort into it.

Additionally, if there is someone in your field whose endorsement of your book would mean the world to you, then it's worth pursuing. This is especially true if you know the person, they're a mentor of yours, or you know someone who could make a connection that you could leverage as a reason to get them to write a foreword for you. Writing a foreword takes considerable time, so it's a big ask. The person writing the foreword will need to read your book to be able to say something meaningful about it. So if you decide to look for someone to write your foreword, ask them if they're willing to do this huge favor for you even before you have your draft finished, and then make sure you give them a minimum of a month to read through the full draft and write the foreword.

As helpful as it could be to have someone's endorsement in the form of writing a foreword for your book, it's certainly not necessary (you'll notice that this book doesn't have one). If you can't think of anyone to ask to write a foreword for you, or if you get turned down by a few different people, then it's probably not worth pursuing. You don't need to have a foreword to meet your business book goals. You could focus your energy instead on getting a few different marketing blurbs for the back cover or getting a few important experts to write book reviews for you, for example.

Chapter 8

MESSY IS BETTER THAN PERFECT

When I warn against overthinking your writing, I'm primarily concerned about the belief that your first draft (or your outline) needs to be perfect. Here's the remedy to this bit of overthinking: make getting to a messy first draft your number-one goal.

In Chapter 4, I asked you to think about perfectionism and other obstacles to getting your first draft out of your head and down on the page. Personally, I have never been very good at writing rough drafts. Whenever I wrote a college essay or philosophy paper, I expected the thing to fall, fully formed, out of my brain—like a baby giraffe crashing out of the womb.

Earlier I shared that I'm a recovering overplanner. This was my writing process for years:

- I would spend hours and days outlining and ideating with myself, my pen, and my legal pads—so many legal pads. By the time I was finished, my outlines almost

looked like handwritten rough drafts because they were
so detailed, except that I didn't use complete sentences.
I would end up with pages of notes.

- Then I would spend hours and days using my notes to
write and edit the draft itself on my computer (using
Microsoft Word—while obsessively hitting save every
30 seconds). Inevitably, most of that time was spent
writing the first third or half of the paper because I
would write a paragraph, then rewrite the same paragraph dozens of times until it was "perfect." I could
easily spend hours on a single sentence, writing, then
editing, then writing before moving onto the next one.

- I always started with the introduction. I felt a compul-
sion to get the introduction "right" before I could move
on to fleshing out the body of the paper. I often spent
days trying to get the introduction right.

- I also did my research as I was writing. So I might write
a few sentences, then fall down a rabbit hole reading
about the finer points of Aristotle's use of the Greek term
este. Research was one of my main procrastination
mechanisms back then. I enjoyed the research more than
the writing because I was more confident in my research
abilities than in my ideating abilities. It's always easier
to read someone else's arguments than to puzzle through
your own.

- Then, often with only a couple of hours left before the
deadline, I would hurriedly write the rest of the paper
and dash off a conclusion without much thought at all.

- I was lucky if I had even 30 minutes (not to mention the
courage) to reread the whole paper and catch any typos
before printing it off to hand in.

In those days, my first draft was really my only draft. And getting that draft written was a miserable, tedious, anxiety-inducing process fueled by perfectionism, fear, imposter syndrome, overthinking, and a severe lack of confidence in my own ideas and writing ability. And most of the time, the results were less than stellar. I'm still not sure how I managed to write a whole dissertation over the course of two years using this process. Since then, I've learned a completely different writing process. It's messy, and it's so much better than perfect.

Much of my penchant for writing perfection comes from how I learned to write. I didn't experience a lot of support or encouragement about my writing after I graduated from high school. (I also didn't get much writing training in high school. I didn't write my first essay until my first semester of college, and the learning curve was steep, to say the least.) If you've also had a less-than-supportive writing experience with your English 101 professor, you might have a similar writing process to what I describe above. And even if all of your writing experiences in school were positive, you may still tend toward perfectionism in your writing. This is true, by the way, even if you feel entirely confident in your ability to speak or share ideas in other forms.

There's something about putting pen to paper or fingers to keyboard that changes the way we express ourselves. This can be a good thing. Writing forces us to think more slowly, and we do a lot of thinking in the process of forming our words on the page. But the act of writing can also force us out of our conversational tone. This can make our writing feel stilted or overly formal and lends itself to perfectionist tendencies.

TIPS FOR AVOIDING PERFECTIONISM

Here are some tips for avoiding this particular overthinking trap as you write your business book:

1. **Write quickly.** It might not feel comfortable at first, but if you push yourself to write as quickly as possible (hitting your word count), it cuts down on overthinking and encourages you to write without a filter. When you're focused on getting the words out, you'll be less focused on making them sound perfect. This can lend itself to a more conversational tone too.

2. **Write out of order.** Instead of trying to write the introduction first, save it for last, and instead of trying to write each chapter in order, write the easiest chapters first. Writing is not a linear process because thinking is rarely a linear process. If you get stuck, stop working on that part and move to something that's easy for you to write so you can keep your momentum going (and hit your word count goal).

3. **Talk through your ideas first.** If you often leave yourself voice memos or enjoy recording yourself talking through ideas, then this is a great way to get your book draft done as well. You can record a series of voice memos, then have them transcribed using AI or a human assistant. I have a hard time processing ideas while I talk, so this method doesn't work well for me. But I do enjoy talking through ideas with friends who enjoy brainstorming with me, and this helps me get past any feelings of stuck-ness I run into.

4. **Separate the research from the writing.** You may find it hard to write quickly before you've done your research, or you may believe you don't know enough about a topic to write about what you think. Hopefully, this is less true, though, since you're writing a business book where much of the content will be

based on your own experiences working with your clients. Still, there may be chapters or sections where you want to talk to other experts or "bone up" on your knowledge. It's fine to do some preliminary research, but it's important to put some guardrails around this: avoid falling down any unhelpful rabbit holes, make sure you're not using others' writing as a crutch, and don't research during writing time (i.e., if you have scheduled an hour to write, research needs to fall outside of that hour).

THE MESSY WRITING PROCESS I RECOMMEND

If you agree that a messy first draft is better than perfect, I recommend that you follow this process to get your first draft finished:

- Take some time to outline your book (as described in the previous chapter). Having a solid outline from the jump will help you write a better first draft, so don't rush this initial bit of writing.
- Do some experimenting as needed and set your word count goal (as described in the previous chapter).
- Quickly write your first draft. Once you have your outline, it's go time. You already have your word count goal, so stick to it. Push yourself to write quickly, write out of order (leave the introduction for last), and talk it out if that's helpful. There may be gaps, and those can be filled in later. Leave yourself notes as needed and keep moving forward. The important thing is to make progress.

- Once you've reached your target word count (e.g., 40,000 words), it's time to edit. This is the fun part! Now you get to fix everything that was needling you in the draft stage and fill in any gaps.

You don't have your English 101 teacher breathing down your neck with an end-of-semester deadline to turn in a 20-page research paper (thank the gods!). And I know that no matter what, a self-imposed deadline will never feel like that (not even Maude can generate the pressure I felt from college essay deadlines). But if you stick to this messy writing process, you will get your book done in record time. Before you know it, it will start to feel like a game, and you'll get a lot of satisfaction out of hitting those word count goals (at least this has been my experience).

Six months (12 weeks to get your rough draft finished plus 12 weeks to edit) is quite impressive and realistic for most business owners who are ready to prioritize writing a business book. But you could also aim for four months (eight weeks to get your rough draft finished plus eight weeks to edit) or even 80 days (six weeks to get your rough draft finished plus six weeks to edit) if you want to push yourself. The messy first draft is the way.

How about no more sheepishly posting on social media that the book you wanted to get done is behind schedule? How about no more wishing you could make the time to write your book? How about setting some word count goals and getting that messy first draft done? Consider how freeing that will feel.

Chapter 9

FORGET ABOUT THE MECHANICS OF WRITING (AND "GOOD WRITING")

Continuing with the perfectionism theme, another way to overthink your writing is to get bogged down in the mechanics of writing. You may have a lot of questions about the mechanics. How many chapters do I need? How long should my paragraphs be? Should I use the Oxford comma, or nah?

Again, these are good questions to ask of an editor (or a friend with some writing chops), but answering these questions should not stop you from diving into writing your first draft. If you can set aside questions about the mechanics of writing for later, your book will be better for it. I know it can be hard. Feel free to research any particularly thorny grammar questions that are bugging you during your non-writing time (some people love Grammarly for this, and Google is my best friend when it comes to grammar questions), but whatever you do, do not let the mechanics of writing become a distraction or keep you from hitting your word count goal.

Keep in mind that there is no magic formula for writing a best-selling book or for "good writing." Feel free to lean on what you consider to be "good writing" and let that be your guide. No matter what book marketers tell you, you don't need to follow any particular writing conventions. I usually recommend knowing the rules so that you can intentionally break them. What is most important is to have an interesting writing style that conveys what you want your reader to know. So try not to worry about whether you're doing it "right."

Will what you're writing help your target audience? That's the only question you need to answer.

WHAT APPS SHOULD I USE?

I don't have a list of recommended apps to offer, though I'm sure you could find as many opinions about this as minutes in a day. I don't have a "tech stack" for writing business books (it's more like a tech pancake). What I use is very simple: Google Docs for writing and Google Drive for organizing my writing. As I write, I use the OneLook Thesaurus or WordHippo, and I often google words I don't know how to spell. Earlier, I mentioned some mind mapping apps I've played with, but I prefer the analog version using note cards or an oversize piece of paper and a pen or marker. I create my outline in Google Docs, and then I open a separate document where I write the first draft. I also edit the same document. If I'm editing in collaboration with my client or an editor, then I'll use the Suggesting feature to make my recommended changes and write comments along the way.

I prefer Google Docs to Microsoft Word or other content creation apps because it automatically saves my changes (you will never lose your work), I can look back in the history to see previous drafts and stuff I've deleted, and I can easily share drafts with others, and they can easily give me feedback using the Suggesting and Commenting features.* You do need to have an internet connection to work online in Google Docs, but you can also set it to write offline, which can be handy when you are traveling and want to write on a plane, for example. It won't autosave when you're writing offline, though, so you have to remember to manually save your work. I find Google Docs to be more intuitive than using Word, but they have basically the same functionality (the current version of Word even allows you to edit the same version with others and see real-time changes; it also autosaves as long as you have it linked to Microsoft's cloud storage, OneDrive), and there's no reason for you to change what you do if it works for you.† When it comes to tech, I am all about simplicity. I don't want to start using something that will distract me from the real task at hand.

Feel free to use Grammarly or something similar to catch the big grammatical errors that weigh you down. But if Grammarly becomes a distraction, feel free not to use it. I don't use Grammarly because it's not perfect (though I've heard good things about the recent AI updates), and I will get distracted at points where I disagree with its recommendations. It's easier for me to simply open up a new Google Doc and go to town. I find the grammar suggestions in Google Docs less distracting, and I know I or an editor can fix any grammar mistakes during the editing phase.

Also, because I'm not precious about my writing, I don't stress over a couple of grammar mistakes. Nearly every book I read has mistakes (this book probably has some), and I don't find that it takes away from my experience as a reader. If you feel strongly about writing a book with zero typos or grammatical errors, then you'll want to hire

---

* I have found that most publishers prefer the manuscript to be delivered in Microsoft Word, but it's easy enough to download a Google Doc in Word, clean up any formatting issues, and share it.

† My dad wrote a book using Pages, Apple's word-processing program, for instance.

a proofreader in addition to an editor (more on the types of editors in Chapter 10). Accept that you're likely too close to your own writing to catch everything yourself with or without a robot assistant.

HOW TO INCORPORATE RESEARCH

Another question you might have as a new author is about best practices for incorporating research or stories into your writing. You probably don't want to fill your book with pages of analysis or research, and you certainly don't need to do a literature review for your business book. Still, some well-placed research can answer your readers' questions and build your reputation as an expert in your field. Of course, if you're drawing on research from others in what you're writing, you should cite your sources. It's the responsible thing to do. I feel very strongly about transparency, and sharing the legacy of my ideas is one way to honor the teachers and experts who have come before me. I owe a debt of gratitude to those who have influenced my work. I have done my best to document those influences throughout this book. Crediting them for their work is one way for me to show respect for the thought leadership ecosystem they have cultivated.

I've already said that I recommend doing your research after you have a complete rough draft (or after gathering enough research ahead of the writing that you feel good about starting on your draft). The separation of research and writing will ensure that you're sprinkling in research to enhance your idea (like salt and pepper enhance a meal) rather than relying on research to make your point for you. Writing without research will allow you to flesh out your idea fully without too much external influence. This way you'll feel confident your idea is truly yours.

There will be times when you'll feel like you can't complete your thoughts until you do some research, though, and that's okay. Focus on keeping your idea in the driver's seat. Do minimal research while writing your first draft. When you find a point you want to dive into more deeply, make a note for yourself and move on. This draft that I'm working on now is littered with comments to my future self. I have a lot of little things to look up, chase down, and bring into the text, but once I finish my draft, I'll have more perspective on each of those little thought bubbles. It should be clear by now, but this method is all about not letting anything stand in the way of getting to your complete, messy draft as quickly as your schedule allows.

Chapter 10

FIX IN THE EDIT

I've said it more than once, but I find editing to be the most enjoyable part of the writing process. There's always some angst and doubt when I'm writing that messy first draft. The pressure to write quickly can start to weigh on me after a while, and that's just the opening that my inner critic is ready to pounce on. Will it be good enough? Do I really have anything interesting to say about this topic? Will people take me seriously? Maybe I'm just a hack, and people are finally going to see me for the fraud I am.

Then, once I break through, fiercely ignoring that inner critic ("No, Maude, *you're* the fraud!"), suddenly those negative voices get super quiet. When that complete draft is staring back at me and I've shown that smug, blinky little cursor who's boss, all of that angst and doubt seems to just melt away. Plus, I've done this enough to trust the process. Usually, when I reread what I've written, I come away thinking it's better than I remember, and then I get excited about the possibility of making it even better through the editing process. When I put my idea in the driver's seat, I believe that what needs to come forth will reveal itself (it's the closest I come to believing in magic, truly).

A lot of creativity comes when you aren't trying to edit yourself as you go. And then a lot of creativity comes from adding in the constraints of sequence, length, logic, etc., in the editing. The writing process needs both of these elements. This means you get double the creativity!

So what is the next step after you have your messy first draft in front of you? What does it look like to fix what you've written in the edit?

FIRST, REREAD THE WHOLE MANUSCRIPT

The first thing I do here, usually after taking at least a few days away from the book, is reread the whole manuscript from start to finish (you can see from my book timeline that I did this two months after finishing the messy first draft of this book). I make more comments in my Google Doc throughout as I go along and take notes in a separate place, like my trusty spiral-bound notebook, but I try to restrain myself from making any substantial changes to the document itself as I'm doing my first pass-through. This is not easy. By this point I'm really itching to edit myself, but I know that editing before I've read through the whole manuscript is inefficient. It means I'll edit one paragraph, then read two more paragraphs and discover that I've already said what I wanted to say later. Perhaps the sequencing of the paragraphs or chapter sections needs to be adjusted, but I can't know that until I've made a complete pass through of the whole chapter, at least. My goal during the first rereading is to get a fresh perspective on the whole thing before I start killing off my darlings.*

---

* Ooh, here's one fun little rabbit hole I went down while writing this book. According to a *Slate* article entitled "Who Really Said 'You Should Kill Your Darlings'?," this phrase has been attributed to Allen Ginsberg, William Faulkner,

Then, I write a wish list of big questions to answer. For example:

- Does the introduction include all and only the most important parts?
- Is this [big theme] clear and running throughout the manuscript?
- Does this idea really belong in this chapter? Should it come in a later chapter?
- Do I need to add cross-references anywhere?
- Are there any bits and pieces that are speaking to a different audience from my target audience?
- Are there any gaps that I need to close?
- Is there anything extraneous that I should cut?
- Where do I need stronger transitions?
- Am I being too repetitive here? Should I repeat this idea there?
- Is anything unclear? How can I clarify the point?

In addition to making sure I answer each of these questions to my satisfaction, I make a "punch list" of things that I want to add or change: pieces that need to be smoothed out or edited down, sections where I need to add meat on the bone, and threads that I want to see running throughout. This is where I list the bits of research I want to include or ideas that I need to chase down and fold into the draft along with any other changes I know I want to make. It will include things that I want to change as well as feedback from others.

Oscar Wilde, Eudora Welty, G.K. Chesterton, Anton Chekhov, and Stephen King (I actually just read this line in King's memoir). But the earliest known example comes from Arthur Quiller-Couch in his 1914 lecture called "On Style." Here's the full quote: "If you here require a practical rule of me, I will present you with this: Whenever you feel an impulse to perpetrate a piece of exceptionally fine writing, obey it—whole-heartedly—and delete it before sending your manuscript to press. *Murder your darlings.*"

Once I have my punch list, I make the changes and methodically check items off my list. For the most part, I go through this list in order, but just as with writing the first draft, I skip the changes I want to make to the introduction, saving those for last. I also try not to stop editing in the middle of a chapter. So for each editing session, I'll try to make all of the changes in one chapter before moving onto the next chapter, and I try to do at least one chapter per work session. Still, it's important to be flexible with this. If you get stuck on something that you can't see a way to fix, it might be a good idea to move on to something else or take a break. Let your subconscious work on the problem. Problems always seem easier to deal with after a good night's rest (this advice works just as well in interpersonal relationships as it does in your relationship with your writing, by the way). You can also lean on your support system for help here. Try talking through the sticking point with a trusted friend. Or ask them to read the bit you're stuck on and brainstorm with you about it. Tag teaming your writing is another strategy that will help you get across the finish line.

Finally, after I get through my whole punch list, which usually takes at least two or three weeks, I take another break from the book before rereading the whole thing one more time. This will be my second round of revisions, only here I'm expecting to be cleaning up only small things. All the big problems have been ironed out by this point. I've done the research I needed to do. What's left might be small word changes or smoothing out sentences that trip me up or feel awkward. The whole editing process could take up to a month or a couple of months if you want. The great part is that while drafting your manuscript can feel like a slog and a race to get those ideas out as quickly as you can, once you've done the hard work of creating, you can afford to take your time with editing. This is the point at which you can let yourself indulge if you like. There can be something very satisfying about slowing down and watching how your brain unpacks the words on the page.

HIRING AN EDITOR

Many of my ghostwriting clients ask me, "Do I need to hire an editor?" My answer: "You definitely want another set of eyes on your manuscript before it gets published." There's no substitute for working with a professional editor. But whether you need to hire an editor yourself depends on how you plan to publish your book. For example, if you work with a traditional publisher, they have in-house editors who work with all of their authors.

There are three basic types of editor: a developmental editor, a copy editor, and a proofreader. Developmental editors help you fix content, structure, flow, and tone. They get into the sausage with you and wring out every last great idea. Copy editors go line-by-line to check things like style, grammar, and spelling. Proofreaders come in at the very end, once your book is formatted for print, to catch any last errors that only someone who is reading your book for the first time would be able to catch. If you go the traditional publishing route or use a hybrid publisher, you'll likely work with all three of these types of editors unless you choose to opt out.

A lot of self-published authors write their first draft, edit it at least a few times themselves, then send it to a copy editor or proofreader to clean up any typos or grammatical errors. This is a fine process. But I think what's even more important than copy editing or proofreading (keeping in mind that I may be more lax about grammatical errors than you are) is a good developmental editor. So even if you don't want to spend a lot of money to get your book written and published, consider making a developmental editor your one big investment if you write your book yourself and decide to self-publish.

A developmental editor will give you a full, substantial, and structural edit. Like an interior designer for your book, your editor will jump inside the architecture with you and help you "renovate" the book according to your goals. Once you've edited your messy draft to your satisfaction, it's time to bring in an editor.

Another reason I recommend a developmental editor, when you're writing your own book, is that depending on your goals and preferences, often working with a good developmental editor will be as good as working with a copy editor and proofreader. Speaking from experience, it's hard to read an entire manuscript and not catch typos or inconsistencies. They often jump off the page at me. This means that after your book has gone through developmental editing, you might feel it's ready for publication. Still, I explicitly tell clients my developmental editing services do not include copy editing or proofreading. Like you, your developmental editor may be too close to the writing to catch every error.

Whether you need a developmental editor, a copy editor, a proofreader, or all three depends on your strengths as well as what you care about the most. Again, I can't recall the last time I read a book with zero grammatical errors or even typos, and many of those books had proofreaders. So to me, as long as I have a good developmental editor who can help me make sure my ideas flow and set the hearts of my readers on fire with my words, I'm not bothered by a misplaced comma or a few small errors that most readers won't even notice. But again, you might feel differently. You do you.

BETA READERS

The final step in the editing process is to send your book to some beta readers. I recommend asking no more than three to five people you trust to be beta readers. Too many early readers can lead to a lot of confusion. You're bound to start getting conflicting advice at some point, and you'll need to make some difficult decisions. Especially if your beta readers don't understand your target reader well, you could end up distracted by the feedback you receive. There is a point where too many cooks really can spoil the broth. So choose your beta readers wisely.

Additionally, you'll want to prepare a set of questions to ask your beta readers. You should feel free to ask whatever you think would be most helpful to you, but here is a list of suggested questions:

- What are your three biggest takeaways from reading this book?
- What did you most appreciate about the book?
- What did you find confusing?
- Who do you think would most benefit from reading this book?
- What would make this book better?

You may notice that none of the above questions can be answered with a "yes" or "no." This is by design because you will only get useful information with open-ended questions.

As an incentive to help you out, you can offer your beta readers free copies of your book in exchange for their feedback and make sure that you give them a month or so to read the book and send you their comments. For best results, these should be readers who you consider to be in your target audience or who know your target reader well. Be careful about sharing your book with other authors simply because they've also written a book. Do they have experience writing books in your book's genre? Do you like the style with which they write? Have they generally shared useful information with you when you have asked?

What do you do with their feedback? Getting feedback will certainly make your book better, but it can also make your book worse or take it in a direction that you don't want. So it is a good idea to stay grounded in your own picture of what you want your book to be and take all the feedback you receive with a grain of salt. Apart from your beta readers, you do not need to listen to absolutely everyone who takes it upon themself to share feedback. Unsolicited advice is often just another distraction. With any feedback you receive, you should ask yourself two questions:

1. Would I seek out this person for their feedback?
2. How well do they understand my target reader?

If the answers are "no" and "not well," then you can comfortably dismiss whatever they say. As you sift through the usable comments you receive, pay special attention to significant points on which more than one person agrees. But don't overlook outliers that ring true to you as well.

One of the challenges with having friends read your book once it's complete is that they may hold back on criticizing the book because they don't want to hurt your feelings. They know how much work you've put in, so even if a question arises in their mind, they may dismiss it, thinking that you must know better.

For this reason, I recommend that you talk about your book early and often. It's easier to get honest feedback early in the process, and it's easier if you ask specific questions (e.g., "My audience believes x, y, and z. Do you think this chapter responds adequately to each of those beliefs?") rather than asking for general feedback (e.g., "Thoughts?"). But you can also reassure your beta readers that you want their honest feedback on the full manuscript. This is their job. There are no stupid questions. Explain to them that you are too close to the writing to be able to identify its flaws. Promise that they are doing you a favor by not holding back on their criticisms. Then, when the criticisms come, remember that your book will be better when it addresses their challenges.

Finally, reading feedback, even when most of it is positive, can be a challenge. (When I was a professor, I would put off reading my student evaluations for as long as possible. Anonymous feedback can be especially brutal.) Try to have a thick skin and intend to read the comments as objectively as possible. Here again, thinking of your edited manuscript as a minimal viable product (MVP) can take the sting out of any criticism you receive. You can always share the feedback you receive with your developmental editor or someone else in your support system to get a gut check too. Another good tip is to read through the criticisms in one sitting, like ripping off a Band-Aid, without reacting. Later on, you can come back with a clear head and decide how to address each one. Above all, try not to take any criticism personally. This is an opportunity to improve your book before you publish it. It's not a commentary on your strengths or weaknesses as a business owner, a writer, or anything else.

Part 3

POSITIONING, PUBLISHING, AND PROMOTING

Once you've written your way across what you think is the finish line and are ready to publish, you might believe you've reached the end of your race. Writing a complete manuscript can feel like running a marathon, but it's more like running one leg of a relay race. At this point, you've planned your business book, and you've written your business book, so you can think of yourself as two-thirds of the way through your race. And just like with a real relay race, you can pass the baton to others who can help you get across the actual finish line (like your publisher). One thing's for sure, though: if you rush the end of the process (or try to take shortcuts), you will be disappointed in the results. To get the outcome you want, like any good athlete knows, you should store up some energy to get across the real finish line. What comes next? Positioning, publishing, and promoting.

Although book sales are probably not your main goal because you recognize the value in writing a business book is actually in being able to reach more clients who need your help, establishing you as a big idea expert, and gaining visibility, you still need to put a lot of effort into positioning, publishing, and promoting your book. In fact, it's best if you can be thinking about these during the planning and writing phases too. The trap here is thinking that you don't need to do any of that—believing the "If you build it, they will come" myth.

TRAP #3: UNDERTHINKING THE POSITIONING, PUBLISHING, AND PROMOTING

Just as there's a symbiotic relationship between you and your idea, there is a symbiotic relationship between your book and your business. That means you can think of the marketing for your book as part of the marketing for your business. Of course your book is a marketing piece for your business. Besides people discovering you through your book, you can pull endless marketing messages from your book and use your book as inspiration for new thought leadership content for years to come. From this perspective, there's an argument to be made that writing a book is the most powerful piece of marketing you could ever do for your business.

Yes, there's a lot your book will do for you when it comes to marketing your business, but to get the most out of your efforts, it's important to recognize that you also need to do your part to market your book, thinking of it as you would any other new product, service, or other income stream you might develop. The right positioning strategy can mean the difference between selling 300 copies (the average number of print copies sold) and selling 3,000 copies or more. Getting your publishing plan right can mean avoiding years of frustration while your book gathers digital dust in a file hidden away from the world. The right promotional strategy can mean getting your book in front of the audiences that will propel you onto the big stages you're hungering for. So this third and final stage in the process is worth thinking about, strategizing for, and planning for even before you start writing.

In truth, I have written this book out of order. You should at least start thinking about the positioning, publishing, and promoting parts of the process even before you start fleshing out your messy first draft. In fact, there's no such thing as starting too early when it comes to marketing your book. And you should continue to work on these pieces throughout the writing process (it can be a good break and a way to keep moving forward on the days when the words aren't flowing). As you continue to read, my reasoning behind these points will become clearer to you.

Chapter 11

POSITIONING

When I talk about marketing your book, what comes to mind? You probably think about tasks like creating social media posts, sharing the Amazon preorder link with your email list, and asking readers to leave you a positive review. But you may not think about positioning or where your book fits in among other books in the same category. When it comes to marketing and promoting your book, positioning is often overlooked. This is a missed opportunity because positioning is a chance to get more of the right eyeballs on your book. That's why I want to start this "third leg of the race" by discussing positioning.

With the right positioning, marketing your book will be easier. You'll have a better idea of what will attract your target readers on social media. You'll feel more confident when you share the link to your book because you'll have more of the right people on your list. And you'll get more positive reviews because your book will be found by those who need the transformation you're offering. If your book ends up with the wrong positioning and in a misleading category, it can hurt distribution. If you don't get specific enough about the audience you are marketing to, then your marketing copy could fall flat. So it's worth thinking about how you want to position your book.

WHAT IS POSITIONING?

Positioning is all about how you want your readers to see your book relative to other similar books. When I started writing this book, I had a clear picture of what I *didn't* want my book to be. So many books about how to write a book are written by writers, for writers. They're full of deeply technical information or advice that can distract you from the real work here, writing the best book you can write within the constraints that you have as a business owner. I wanted to write a book testing the truth and the practicality of the conventional wisdom and sharing where it doesn't pass the smell test based on my clients' and my experiences. This book isn't for everyone, and that's good. That's positioning.

GET TO KNOW YOUR COMPETITION: LOOK AT OTHER BOOKS IN YOUR SPACE

Your first stop is to get the lay of the land. You may remember that back in Part 2, I warned against feeling like you need to read the top ten books (or more!) you see as close competitors. This is because I didn't want you to get lost in research, lose your core idea, or lose your nerve, feeding your brain's penchant for comparing your messy first draft to someone else's finished product. But it's a good idea to know roughly where your book will sit on the virtual shelves. So now that you're at the positioning, publishing, and promoting stage, it's time to get to know your competition.

To get a good idea, familiarize yourself with the most popular books in the genre or category you suspect is best for your book (e.g., business development and entrepreneurship, marketing and sales, management and leadership, investing, personal finance). Again, this doesn't necessarily mean reading every word of every book. But you can at least do a search on Goodreads, Amazon, and Barnes & Noble to see what's out there and take a look at the book blurbs, summaries, and tables of contents for each relevant specimen. You can also learn a lot from the book's website or sales page. How are they marketing the book? Is the audience the same as yours? What are the relevant differences?

Next, try to get specific. Having a strong niche will help those who need the transformation your book offers find it. Consider how your book is different from other books in the same genre. If you have a picture in your mind of the type of person who might read another consultant's book, for example, think about how your audience might differ. For instance, one consultant may specialize in business development strategy while you might focus on messaging, marketing, and sales training. This way, you can position your book relative to other well-known books in the same genre.

You can also differentiate your book by thinking about where in their journey your ideal reader would pick up your book. Are you writing to pre-revenue start-up founders? Or founders running growth-stage companies making at least $1 million in revenue that are looking to raise Series C funding? Even if your book would be helpful for founders at all stages, it's better, from a marketing perspective, to position your book as being for a more specific audience. That will ensure that your marketing messages are clear, feel more targeted, and thus create the impression that your book is more helpful. You never need to worry about excluding certain people because your description is too specific. You only need to worry about creating vague marketing descriptions that confuse potential readers. Again, positioning should make your marketing efforts easier and give you a better return on your investment.

Of course, the earlier you think about positioning, the better. But there are also a lot of ways to play with positioning after your book manuscript is nearly complete. Positioning can be as simple as what you write in your book summary or what you choose as the title for your book. Still, you want to make sure that your book delivers on the promises you make in any marketing or promotional material you share. That's why it's best to think about positioning early on—if not from the very beginning, then before you finish your messy first draft.

For my book ghostwriting clients, I do research into their audience and what books they enjoy and why. I look into the value offered by similar books in the genre and point out gaps in the market I think my client's book could fill. Pro tip: Amazon's one-star reviews are a gold mine for discovering these gaps in the market.

For example, when I worked with a wealth advisor and money coach to write a book about money mindset, positioning was especially important. There are thousands of books written every year about money mindset, so the question we asked was "How could we set her book apart from those others?" Well, this book was written specifically for women (which doesn't narrow down the audience by much—the majority of money books are written for women); it was targeted for professional women (ages 40–65), in the workforce but approaching retirement, who by all external accounts would be considered wealthy but whose minds haven't caught up to this fact yet. The book we wrote was about shifting that mindset. Because this is a very specific topic, there are many fewer books written targeting this particular audience, which is a good thing. This really narrowed down the audience and gave us clear positioning.

A lot of new authors think the best way to position themselves is to appeal to as broad an audience as possible (a bigger audience means more book sales, right?), but in reality, you want to speak to a narrow audience. It's not that people who don't fall into that specific category won't pick up your book; it's just that positioning your book for a narrower audience means you have a better chance of capturing the eyes of those who will benefit the most and sing your praises. When you think about it, the population of readers who are both (a) open to listening to your idea and (b) ready to make the transformation you're offering is likely in the thousands. Concentrate on finding those folks and you'll have mastered positioning.

GET TO KNOW YOUR AUDIENCE: ASK WHAT PEOPLE WANT TO READ

Besides doing research about the current books available on the market, it's a good idea to do some market research for your book as well. I discussed this back in Chapter 5 when I asked you to validate your big idea. This is an important piece of the feedback puzzle and is the very start of your marketing plan. You never know what you'll learn in these early exploratory discussions, and you shouldn't assume that you know what your readers are looking for. Perhaps you're thinking about writing a comprehensive book spanning your entire book topic, but when you do your research, you find that your target audience isn't interested in buying a reference book. Instead, they are hungry for information about a specific subtopic. It may be a subtopic that has been neglected by others in your industry, leaving a gap that you can fill. This is important to know before you get too far into writing your messy first draft.

Gaining a better understanding of how to position your book requires a process similar to what I recommended for validating your book idea. To do your market research around positioning your book, come up with three to five questions you want to ask your target readers. Then find five to ten people in your target market to invite for a 20- or 30-minute interview. Ideally, these interviewees shouldn't be your clients, because they are already acclimated to your way of working, so they're somewhat biased. You'll get the most useful information from ideal readers outside of your immediate circle (plus, being part of the conversation will make them excited to buy your book when it's published), but it's okay to start with people in your network. People are usually very open to helping with this type of research, but you can also sweeten the deal by offering them a free or discounted copy of the book once it's published, or you could offer another incentive, like a free consultation.

Here are some sample questions to ask your target readers:

- What is the one big question you have about [your book's topic]?
- What do you struggle with the most when it comes to [your book's topic]?
- What other books on [your book's topic] have you read?
- What did you find most useful about those books?
- What did you notice was missing in those books?
- If I could wave a magic wand and solve one problem for you in relation to [your book's topic], what would it be?
- What do you see as the biggest benefit to solving that problem?

Again, you can see why it would be helpful to do this kind of market research ahead of writing your book, but even after you've written it, the answers to these questions will be helpful as you consider how you talk about your book. It's not likely that you will get answers that contradict what you've written, so there's no risk in getting to know your audience better at any stage in the process.

Chapter 12

CHOOSING A TITLE

Getting to know your competition and your audience will also help you with one of the most important elements of positioning: choosing a title.

Many authors seem to get their book idea when a title comes to them (in a dream—it often seems to come in a dream). So you may know your title even before you begin writing. If this is the case for you, great. You can skim through this chapter to make sure your title isn't wildly off base and focus on other chapters. But one warning: if you read something here that makes you think your title is "wrong," think again. I want to encourage you not to change your title—especially if you feel a strong, personal connection to it—based on a whim (including a whim that comes to you because of something I've written here). No publishers predicted that a book called *Zen and the Art of Motorcycle Maintenance* would sell millions of copies, yet that's exactly what happened.*

---

* Robert Pirsig's manuscript was rejected 121 times, though the book's editor, James Landis, wrote, "The book is brilliant beyond belief. It is probably a work

Whenever you have a gut feeling about a particular title, that's something to pay attention to. I once worked with a client who had an idea for a title that was slightly racy but catchy and perfect for a book geared toward empowering women to build their own wealth. She was worried that readers might take offense, though (she has lived in the South her whole life). I encouraged her to go with the sexy, memorable title, and she did. It was a smart move and gave her a lot to play with in marketing her book. Were potential readers offended? We'll probably never know if they were (to my knowledge, though, no one has ever offered anything other than praise for her title). What we do know is that whenever she shares the title, she gets some chuckles, and many have told her they bought the book because of the title. So change a title that you really love only if you have an excellent reason.

If a fully formed, catchy title (sexy or not) did not pop into your head on day one, fear not. Personally, I always settle on my titles last. As I'm writing, title ideas bubble up, and when they do, I make note of them. They're sometimes catchy phrases or phrases that I find myself repeating throughout the book. I keep a running list of working titles at the top of my manuscript and add to it whenever an idea strikes me. Currently, I have at least ten possible titles at the top of this document. Eventually I'll hit on my title or something close that I can continue playing with and sharing with others for feedback.

For this book, here are the criteria I came up with for my title and subtitle:

- I wanted a one-word title that had a light, easy tone— easy (like Sunday morning).

---

of genius and will, I'll wager, attain classic status." He was right (https://lithub.com/the-most-rejected-books-of-all-time).

- I wanted that one word to be memorable and searchable (i.e., easy to find with a Google search).
- I wanted the whole title and subtitle to be subtly funny (or something that I, at least, think is funny)—not sure my title meets this criterion.
- I also wanted it to include keywords such as "thought leadership," "business book," and "big idea expert."

But I didn't start out with any of this. I started by writing down any turn of phrase or idea that came to me. It pays not to edit yourself in these cases. When an idea comes, write it down. You need to dig through the rough to get to the diamond.

I also wanted that one-word title to be rebellious, paradoxical, and on brand for me. And once "unwritten" popped into my head, I couldn't let it go, so I knew it had to be the title. I briefly considered "bookish" too but ultimately rejected it because I was worried that it wouldn't appeal as much to business owners as to academics and recovering academics (not my main audience). Then I had a string of different subtitles and continued to play with them throughout the writing process. Once I hit on *Unwritten: The Thought Leader's Guide to Not Overthinking Your Business Book*, I knew I found my title.

CONVENTIONAL WISDOM ABOUT CHOOSING TITLES

Yes, your title matters. Despite my suggestion above that you should feel a connection to your title, you shouldn't just go with your gut here. Your title is the first thing someone will learn about your book, and it's always good to have a title that is both memorable and searchable so that when others mention to their friends that they're reading your book, they can say the title out loud, and their friends can easily go and find the book on Google. This is a good argument for starting with a one-, two-, or three-word title followed by a subtitle. Having a title that's easy for fans to remember and new readers to look up will absolutely help with the marketing and distribution of your book. While a great title alone won't make your book a bestseller, a poor title certainly won't help buyers find it.

There are some conventions to follow with book titles. For example, you want your title to be relatively short (i.e., one, two, or three words). It's best to choose something that gives a preview of what your book is about and piques the interest of your target readers. Then, in the subtitle, you make a promise to the reader or share something that makes it clearer what type of book they're picking up, without giving away too much.

Also, your subtitle should be no longer than 14 words, it should contain some "emotional" words (or appeal to core human values), and you should avoid using words that are overly complicated, confusing, or difficult to pronounce. Use keywords for SEO purposes too. Brainstorm a list of 20 to 50 words or phrases that describe your big idea, then experiment with different ways of putting them together. Once you have a few ideas, do some research to make sure you're not duplicating any of your competitors' titles. While you don't need to have a perfectly unique title, you do want to avoid your book being confused with other business book titles. Simply pull up Amazon and enter your title into the search box to make sure you're in the clear.

If following these conventions clearly improves your title, great—again, consult your gut. But keep in mind that some of the most memorable titles are memorable precisely because they break with conventional wisdom.

Here are some famous business book titles and why they were successful:

Atomic Habits: An Easy & Proven Way to Build Good Habits & Break Bad Ones
by James Clear
    The title is memorable and searchable. The subtitle offers a promise to the reader and a preview of what they'll get in the book. It's basically a one-sentence summary of the book.

Insight: The Surprising Truth About How Others See Us, How We See Ourselves, and Why the Answers Matter More Than We Think
    by Tasha Eurich
    This title actually breaks with conventional wisdom. The subtitle is a whopping 21 words long. But the title "insight" is memorable and searchable. Again, we have a summary of the book in one sentence. It just happens to be a longer sentence, which attracts Eurich's target reader: sophisticated leaders who want to learn more about themselves and go deeper into understanding team dynamics. Whenever I see this title, I wonder if Tasha Eurich herself knows it by heart. I'm guessing she probably does, but I bet it took some practice for it to roll off of her tongue. I haven't yet memorized my book title, but I'll have lots of practice before the book is published.

Grit: The Power of Passion and Perseverance
    by Angela Duckworth
    Again, this title is memorable and searchable. It gives away less of what the book is about than the other titles

we've looked at. Still, it offers a preview of the big concepts the book discusses. It's a short, cute title packing a big punch. Bonus points for alliteration. I adore alliteration.

ON CROWDSOURCING YOUR TITLE

A lot of authors make the mistake of crowdsourcing their titles and then feeling married to whatever the crowd thinks. But the crowd isn't always right. By "crowdsourcing," I should clarify that I mean outsourcing your power by posting on social media or in a group and asking others to give you title suggestions. You might get some interesting suggestions by sharing a synopsis of the book with your audience and seeing what people come up with, or you might be led in a totally wrong direction. I'm not talking about coming up with a few possible titles that you like and asking for feedback. That's actually a *good* idea and something I encourage you to do, but I want you to own the process.

For best results, narrow your title down to your three best options before asking for feedback. You can do this on social media, by sending a survey to your email list, or by asking people whose opinions you trust. At least this way, your steady hand will be involved in choosing the title for your book. And while you might be able to predict which title the crowd prefers, it's always better to get people to explain what about the title they like. That's where you may uncover some surprises that will help you land on the best title. You can also ask them to talk about what associations they have with each title to figure out what impressions readers will have. When someone guesses what your business book is about from your title, then you know you're on to something.

Above all, you want a book title that resonates with you. When I work with my ghostwriting clients, I share possible titles as we work on their book. Typically, the authors themselves will gravitate toward one title, and I'll continue to play with the wording while they also add their own thoughts until we get it right. It's important that you feel ownership over your book title. If an author doesn't feel connected to their title, they're not going to feel connected to their book. And connecting to your book is key for so many reasons. First, it makes the marketing easier. And it keeps your motivation up. If you end up with a title that doesn't speak to you but seems to satisfy a group of random people who happen to see your survey on LinkedIn, you could lose the enthusiasm you once had.

Better than asking a totally random set of people for feedback is to ask your beta readers what they think about your title options. Again, share your top three favorite titles and then ask them to weigh in or to suggest their own if they wish. Having read the whole book, they are in a better position to come up with helpful titles than someone who has simply read a synopsis and thought about it for a few seconds.

Notice that this is not the same advice as "go with your gut." While I do want you to choose a title that resonates with you, I also want you to give it some serious thought. The title that comes to you in a dream may not be the very best title for your book. So whatever you land on, turn your idea over in your mind. If you can't live and breathe your title, then you haven't found it. You'll know when you find it.

CHOOSE SOMETHING THAT CONNECTS WITH YOUR BUSINESS

Finally, since this is a business book, the title should relate to your business. If you have a tagline or a catchy business name, that's a natural place to start. I thought about adding The Pocket PhD to my title, but in the end, it made more sense to take it out. Perhaps there's a statement or phrase you use often with your clients that exemplifies your business or the work that you do. If it's something your clients would recognize as being yours, then consider whether it belongs in your title.

Here's a simple way to jump-start your title brainstorming: Imagine that someone asked you to summarize your book in one sentence. What would that one sentence be? Could you pull the title from that? Keep a running list of all the possibilities (as I mentioned, I keep a list at the top of my manuscript). At some point during the writing process, you'll have your Eureka! moment.

Chapter 13

TRADITIONAL PUBLISHING VS. SELF-PUBLISHING VS. HYBRID PUBLISHING

How to publish your book is a big decision. With every person I've encountered who is serious about writing a book, the publishing question always comes up. What are the options? First, there's the way books have been published basically since the invention of the printing press: through a publisher or press. Traditionally, major publishing houses like Macmillan, Wiley, Simon & Schuster, Penguin Random House, and HarperCollins were the gatekeepers. They decided which books got published and how many books were in circulation. They also decided how many copies would be available for libraries to buy and lend out. Of course, a lot of ink has been spilled about how this gatekeeping is not best for authors, but at one time, this was really your only option for publishing a book.

Largely in response to the concern about gatekeepers, independent (or indie) publishers have come onto the scene. Many indie publishers were started by publishing professionals who wanted to break away from the big publishing houses and do things their own way. This can be a good option, especially if you can find an indie publisher that specializes in your book's genre. They will know the market and can provide information you wouldn't otherwise think to consider, and they more or less follow the traditional publishing model but with terms that are more author-friendly.

The rise of desktop publishing and print-on-demand turned the publishing industry on its head in the 1990s. Especially since Amazon got into the book publishing game, self-publishing has exploded in popularity, and this rise in popularity has also lent more credibility to self-publishing. Even 20 or 30 years ago, self-publishing was considered second-rate. Now, because so many more people are choosing to publish this way, the stigma around it has mostly disappeared, especially when it comes to publishing a business book. You might wonder: What is the point of self-publishing if absolutely anyone can publish a book this way? But you might also wonder: What is the point of giving certain people gatekeeping authority to decide whose books get published? Without a doubt, the democratization of publishing via desktop publishing allows ideas to get into the world that wouldn't have otherwise seen the light of day. That's undoubtedly a double-edged sword (see the publishing stats in the introduction), but overall, I see this as a welcome shift. There are few drawbacks to expanding the marketplace of ideas.

Finally, there is a third way, which offers a blend of traditional and self-publishing. Hybrid publishing has a lot of different modes. Some hybrid publishers sell services for walking first-time authors through the self-publishing process. Others focus on the benefit of helping authors market and distribute their books. So if you have a lot of questions about self-publishing and aren't sure you want to take the time to find the answers yourself, a hybrid publisher could help. Keep in mind that you will pay for these services and all production costs (I am using a hybrid publisher, and my budget is around

$40,000, which also includes a book marketing plan), so you'll want to ensure that you're getting enough bang for your buck. The good news is that you can choose how much you want to spend.

The best way to answer the question of how to publish your book is to consider your goals. Because you aren't looking to sell millions of copies, and you are looking to help others, indie publishing, self-publishing, or hybrid publishing is likely the way to go (this is how most of my clients have chosen to publish their business books), but there are exceptions to this loosely held rule, which I discuss below.

You can also take a look at the other books in your book's genre to get a sense for how most people go about publishing in that space. This will help you get a handle on what your audience might be expecting too. Of course, you can also ask your friends who have published books how they did it and what their experience was. Don't be shy about asking. They're likely eager to share what they've learned (that has been my experience in researching my publishing options). But also be on the lookout for FOMO creeping in and influencing what you see as the best option for you. Your goals may be different from your friends' goals. It's easy to get mesmerized by the shiny objects people dangle in front of you, so make a list of goals and stay grounded in them.

WHEN TO SELF-PUBLISH

Most of the time with my ghostwriting clients, I recommend self-publishing (which includes hybrid publishing). It's faster, easier, and usually sufficient to meet their goals. When you're writing a business book, in most cases, it's best to get your book out there and into the hands of your readers ASAP. You may be worried about getting scooped. You may be too busy to let your book steal too much more of your precious time. You may be itching to help your readers with their big transformations. Because your book is first a marketing piece for your business, how it's published is not as important as your plan for distribution, which we'll discuss below. Above all, I want you to consider that the sooner your book is available, the sooner it can start to grow your business.

I also recommend self-publishing (or indie publishing or hybrid publishing, which I'll discuss below) for 95% of my business book clients because most of the benefits that people believe they'll gain by going the traditional route aren't actually provided by traditional presses. For example, a lot of authors think that publishers take care of the marketing of a book, when in reality, the first question they ask you is "What's *your* plan for pre-selling 5,000-10,000 copies of your book?" To be on the *New York Times* bestseller list, you need to sell at least 7,500 copies of your book in the first week. Your publisher and agent will want to see signs that this is within reach for you. And as you've seen, the average book published in the U.S.—whether self-published or traditionally published—sells 300 copies. So, if you're thinking of going the traditional route, you have to ask yourself if you believe your book is in the top 1–2% of books being sold.

And just in case you think you will aim for a second- or third-tier publisher instead, they will still want to know how you will sell 3,500 copies of your book in the first year. This is not easy if you don't have a sizable audience primed to buy your book, a solid marketing plan, and a distribution strategy. If you do have dreams of writing a bestseller with a traditional publisher, and you have the audience (or are prepared to build it), make sure that you also have a solid marketing and PR plan. Don't get me wrong: your publisher will do some marketing for you (and take care of a lot of other things, like editing, book cover design, and formatting), but they will need to be convinced that you have the reputation and audience to hit their sales projections. In other words, you will need to market your book to publishers and agents before you market it to your audience.

WHEN TO GO THE TRADITIONAL ROUTE

Traditional publishing remains highly selective. Unless you are a widely known CEO, business leader, celebrity, or influencer, it's difficult to convince a traditional publisher to take a risk on you. Because you are a small-business owner, the odds are not in your favor. It's not impossible to break through. It can be done, but I want you to go in with your eyes open.

Now, as I said, if you land a deal with a traditional publisher, they will do some limited marketing for you. They will put your book in their catalog and perhaps send out a blurb to email subscribers. Your book will gain some clout from being under the umbrella of a press that is a household name (e.g., Simon & Schuster, Penguin Random House, and HarperCollins). Plus, your book will be on the shelves of physical bookstores and in airports, which means that readers will discover your book. And traditional publishers do take away some of the headaches that come with editing, formatting, and distributing a book. They'll help you with decisions like choosing the best book cover design (which can make a big difference in the number of sales), and your book will go through an editing process with the publisher. By far, the main advantage here is that you won't have to pay anything up front since the publisher covers all production fees, and you may even get an advance.

But all of this comes at a steep price: the publishing rights to your book and, often, a raw deal when it comes to the percentage of royalties that you get (4–15% is typical). And even before you get to the publishers, you'll need to find an agent who will shop your book around to different publishers. You won't get anywhere reaching out directly to publishers. Agents are another set of gatekeepers in this industry, and the process of finding an agent can take months or years.

Here's the path to traditional publishing:

- You decide you'd like to pitch your book idea to traditional publishers (or, if you have built a solid thought leadership platform, a traditional publisher might reach out and ask if you'd like to write a book).
- You'll need to write a book proposal (or pay someone to write it for you) that includes a marketing plan, information about your author platform, and sample chapters.
- With your book proposal in hand, you'll write query letters to agents.
- Once you find an agent who is ready to pitch your book, they'll probably guide you to make changes to the book proposal.
- When your agent is satisfied with your book proposal, they'll start shopping it around to publishers they believe are a good fit for your book. They will also advise you about any book deal offers you receive.

Going the traditional route can be a difficult road, but it could be right for you. Again, your goals should determine how you publish your book. If you're hoping to be the next Mel Robbins, then you will want to make the traditional route work for you. Just know that each step in the process stands between you and your book getting into the hands of your target readers, and because there's little value to a business book before it's in the hands of readers, it takes a lot to convince me that there's an upside to delaying this outcome.

The bottom line is that traditional publishers and agents are gate-keepers, and while getting past the gatekeepers has its benefits, it's often more work than you realize and takes more time than you expect, and the benefits don't always outweigh the costs.

For all these reasons, traditional publishing is usually not the best choice for business books. However, there are some important exceptions to this rule:

- If you have connections in the publishing industry who you think could help to guide you through the traditional publishing process, and you're willing to reach out to them and make the ask, then it's worth at least testing those waters. At the least, you can get the opinion of an expert who knows the publishing industry better than you do.

- If you have one incredible story or a lot of interrelated jaw-dropping stories, and you could honestly see your book being optioned for a film or being turned into a screenplay, then it's worth pursuing a traditional publisher (you will likely have to sign away your rights to any film options, though).

- If you have already published a book or multiple books with a traditional press, then you know what the process looks like, and you are in a good position to make this call for yourself rather than listening to me. You may disagree with a lot of what I have already said too. If you want to school me, feel free to reach out! I'd love to hear your perspective. Admittedly, I'm a relative newbie to the publishing industry.

- If you are your industry's next Brené Brown, then it's worth finding a traditional publisher. You could actually shoot yourself in the foot if you self-publish first (with the plan to go to traditional publishers later), especially if your book doesn't do exceptionally well. If, on the other hand, you self-publish and sell thousands of copies, you've got some great social proof to take to publishers with your next book.

WHAT'S HYBRID PUBLISHING, AND WHEN IS IT A GOOD OPTION?

Earlier in this chapter, I said hybrid publishers offer you a blend of both the self-publishing and traditional routes. They will guide you through the self-publishing process and deliver many of the perks promised by traditional publishers, such as marketing support, PR opportunities such as readings at local bookstores, and features in industry publications. With hybrid publishers, authors retain all the rights to their own work. These publishers charge an up-front fee (anywhere from $25,000 to $100,000), and most keep some royalties, but the royalty splits are typically better for authors (15–100%) than what traditional publishers offer.

Once you start doing this research for yourself, you will find that every hybrid shop has its own set of rules. So it's important to know what you'll be getting and to shop around before you sign on with any publisher. The old adage stands: if it sounds too good to be true, it probably is.

Also, realize that any results publishers share as benefits of using their services need to be understood within the right context. So someone with an Instagram following of 10,000 is going to have an easier time selling their book than someone with an Instagram following of 300. Make sure when you compare, you're comparing apples to apples. This is also to suggest that many of the variables that factor into an author's results are not attributable to the hybrid publisher. Getting an accurate picture of what they can do for you is key. Distribution is especially important. Publishers often have deals with book distributors, which can also get your book into brick-and-mortar stores or can promise you access to a bigger list than you have on your own. These are benefits that may be worth paying for.

Still, don't automatically assume that you need to go through anyone else in order to get your book out there. Hybrid publishing is essentially self-publishing with support. If you feel good about your ability to manage the project that is positioning, publishing, and promoting your book, then you may be quite happy to do the work largely on your own, pulling in experts only where it makes sense.

HYBRID PUBLISHING VS. INDIE PUBLISHING

Independent publishers can also be a good option. Like hybrid publishers, many of these groups have their own digital publications, platforms, and followers or have deals with popular outlets (e.g., Inc.com, *Forbes*) for reaching your target audience. These types of publishers can be a good option for business book authors, especially indie publishers that specialize in your industry or in your book's genre, because they help you amplify your reach by giving you access to their platforms and letting you borrow their audience.

Indie publishers follow the traditional publishing model but tend to be more author-friendly, though again, you have to do your due diligence and make sure everything is as they promise. This is an unregulated industry, so it's up to you to do your homework so you can protect yourself. Just because a publisher labels itself "indie" doesn't mean that it is the greatest champion of authors. I have found the lines between "hybrid" and "indie" to be quite blurry.

STEER CLEAR OF VANITY PUBLISHERS

There's one more type of publisher to be aware of—so that you can steer clear of them. Unfortunately, vanity presses sometimes dress themselves up to look like hybrid publishers—as in all cases, buyer beware. The main difference between legitimate hybrid publishers and vanity publishers is that whereas hybrid publishers are selective (though less selective than traditional publishers) about which titles they publish, vanity publishers will publish anything, no questions asked. Hybrid publishers also advise authors on aspects like pricing, positioning, and salability. In addition, you should consider whether a publisher is providing concrete, valuable deliverables (e.g., a full edit, a robust marketing plan, a distribution strategy) or simply printing your book or uploading it to Kindle Direct Publishing (KDP), Amazon's system. Vanity publishers offer no benefit to publishing with them. You pay for the privilege of having their name on your book, but unlike with traditional publishers, their name is not worth anything. If you end up with a vanity press, you could spend thousands of dollars for a low-quality book and a lot of headaches. Because self-publishing is a good option, there's really no reason to pay to merely have your book published. You're better off doing it all yourself than falling for what is essentially a scam. So look for these red flags.

Unless you fit one of the exceptions I mention in the traditional publishing section, you will likely want to self-publish your business book. The next question is how much support you want, and then it's a matter of shopping around until you find the process that works for you and fits your budget. If you want to go the self-publishing route, look at books on Amazon to get a feel for what looks good or bad. Order some books and hold them in your hands too, or go to your own bookshelf and get a feel for what you like. From there, you can decide what services you want to invest in to get a high-quality book.

Also, keep in mind that you can hire out the pieces you need rather than spending the big bucks on a turn-key service. For example, you can hire a designer to create a book cover for you, someone else to do your book layout and formatting, and someone else to come up with a marketing plan for you. These types of professional services are worth spending money on because they change the way your book is received by your readers. PR is another good area to invest in because distribution is even more important than publication when it comes to getting your business book into the hands of your readers (more on this when we get to promotion). This piecemeal approach may make more sense than finding one hybrid publisher to do all of those things. But it's worth shopping around and talking to some different service providers since what's best for you depends on the benefits on offer.

Chapter 14

HOW TO MARKET YOUR BOOK: THE MINIMUM VIABLE MARKETING PLAN (MVMP)

As I said at the beginning of Part 3, it's easy for authors to cut corners or to ignore the need to do any marketing. But it's simply not true that if you write it, people will buy it. It's a drag to realize after you've worked so hard to write your book that the real work has only just begun. And I'll go out on a limb and assume that marketing isn't your favorite thing to do, and even if you do love marketing your business, marketing your book probably feels like a whole new beast to slay. But not marketing your book is the biggest mistake you can make. Again, distribution is the most important piece at this stage, and strong distribution depends on strong marketing. You've put in too much work to set your business book on the shelf and forget about it. So let's talk about what the minimum viable marketing plan (MVMP) might look like when it comes to marketing your book.

THE CHALLENGE

I can't emphasize enough that regardless of whether you choose to self-publish or to publish with a press, you will need to market your book. It's tough, though. As a business owner, you already know that marketing is a full-time job. That's why, if you have the means, I recommend you invest in help with this aspect of your business book. There are plenty of people out there who specialize in all aspects of book marketing. Start by surveying those who help you market your business (e.g., copywriters, graphic designers, PR folks). They may offer additional services specifically for books or at least be able to help with the various pieces of marketing content you will need (e.g., a book blurb, social media posts, a page on your website dedicated to the book) at a reasonable price, and if they can't help, they may have referrals to share.

If you have a PR team, they may be able to help set up your book launch and find you opportunities to do press around your book (e.g., podcast guest spots, guest articles). Of course, finding experts who specialize in book marketing will likely yield the best results here, but there's also something to be said for working with a team that already knows you and your brand. Because your book is an extension of your business and your thought leadership ecosystem, the marketing for everything should be cohesive. Your book is a product of your business and should be marketed as such.

You can also DIY your own book marketing. And if you do, you'll want to make sure you have a book marketing strategy ready to be implemented at least three months prior to your book publication date. Aim for a six-month plan covering the three months prior to your book's publication date and three months after your book's publication date. The earlier you begin building buzz around your book, the better chance you have of hitting your goals, and again, it's never too early (or too late) to start.

If you've already published your book and are wondering if you can market it now, the answer is "absolutely." It will be a bit harder to build buzz since you don't have a book launch date to build a marketing campaign around, but you can find other reasons to market your book. Perhaps you have a speaking engagement coming up, or you're hosting an event. Use these as opportunities to talk up your book too.

Your Minimal Viable Marketing Plan (MVMP) for your book should include:

- A strategy for marketing your book (ideally, at least three months in advance of your book publication date)
- A strategy for promoting preorders (ideally, at least a month in advance of your book publication date)
- A strategy for promoting your book launch event (ideally, at least two months in advance)
- A list of people you want to invite to be part of your launch team
- A list of marketing activities you want to ask your launch team to complete for you (e.g., reviews on Amazon, emails to their lists, social media posts, preorders)
- A list of marketing activities you will complete before and after your launch

Of course, to map all of this out, you also need to know some crucial dates:

- The date your book manuscript goes to the printer (if you're not self-publishing)

- The date you'll be ready to print-on-demand (i.e., the day you upload your manuscript if you are self-publishing)
- Your book-in-hand date (date you can begin selling preorders)
- Your official book release date (date preorders end)
- Any book launch events you will host (e.g., book readings, signing events)

In case you're keeping track, I've now mentioned three groups of people you need to gather together: beta readers, target readers to participate in market research, and your launch team. While there can certainly be some overlap, you'll want to make sure you have a deep enough networking bench to support these key groups.

WHAT MARKETING COLLATERAL DO YOU NEED?

To go along with your MVMP plan, you'll need to create all of the content to use to promote your book.

At a minimum, here is what you'll need as marketing collateral:

- A book summary or description: This will be posted on Amazon or wherever your book is for sale and should contain critical marketing messages
- An author bio: This will be posted on Amazon or wherever your book is for sale
- A book webpage: A page on your website dedicated to the book where you can post your summary, author bio, and a link to buy the book, plus promote your launch events and share any bonus content with readers
- Social media posts
- Blog and/or Substack articles

- Graphics to use as event promos (for your book launch and any press events you do)
- Freebies or opt-ins that readers will have access to

MARKETING YOUR BOOK TO A WARM AUDIENCE

You'll want to think about how to market your book to a warm audience—those who know your business, are aware that you're writing a book, and are excited to read it. You can market to this audience in the same way you already market your other products and services to them.

1. Create social media posts about your book. There are at least five different categories of posts you'll want to create for LinkedIn or whatever your main social media channels happen to be:

1. Personal stories about your book and why you're writing it
2. Educational posts with snippets from the key points in the book
3. Teasers with the big themes or biggest takeaways from the book
4. Explainer posts about the key concepts mapped out in the book
5. Exercises that you share in the book or that could be companions to different parts of the book

I've also seen authors create trailers for their books, which are basically promotional videos. These are optional, of course, but can be fun if you're into that kind of thing and have access to the right resources.

It's smart to work on creating these as you're writing, or you can wait until you have your full draft ready before you start pulling out or creating all of these assets. Regardless, you'll need to have some marketing assets ready as soon as you start talking about your book publicly.

You'll be able to repurpose this content in several different ways, so make it easy to find the content to share. Instead of copying and pasting directly from the book and into LinkedIn, for example, create a content calendar or marketing file where you keep each post you make and that you can return to easily. The last thing you want is to comb through all of your LinkedIn posts from the past six months, looking for that marketing blub you came up with in an impulsive moment.

2. **Create email newsletters promoting the book.** You can repurpose the content you create for social media or your blog that touch on the book and use them as email content to share with your list.

3. **Invite them to your events.** Of course, you'll want to invite your warm audience to any and all events related to your book. If you do a book launch event, create promos to share with your current network. If you do any book readings, virtual or in person, invite your audience. Make sure that everyone in your current audience knows that you're writing a book, and let them know well in advance when the book will be available for preorder.

You cannot overpromote your book to your warm audience. Remember, these folks are your superfans. They want to see you do well. You will not annoy them by sharing more often than you think you should be sharing. Keep in mind that you will feel like a broken record, but your audience (perhaps with the exception of your best friend and your mom) does not see every post or read every email. Marketing messages work when they start to feel repetitive.

As I've been writing this book, I sometimes feel as if I'm talking about it too much. I have to remind myself, though, that most of these conversations so far have been happening one-on-one. I also know I'm not talking about it too much because I still hear from people who follow me closely on LinkedIn who say they didn't know I'm writing a book. Whenever I hear this, it's a nudge to do more and better marketing.

MARKETING YOUR BOOK TO A COLD AUDIENCE

You will need to do at least some marketing to a cold audience too. You should spend time building your audience on social media (a good target to shoot for is more than 10,000 connections or followers on LinkedIn) ahead of the book launch. While you shouldn't simply connect with absolutely anyone on LinkedIn, you also shouldn't be too choosy. Ideally, you're connecting with your target readers and people whom your target readers trust. As of this writing, you can connect with 20 people per day or 100 per week on LinkedIn, so do some simple math to see how many connection requests you need to send before your book launch date. For example, when I started writing this book, I had 8,468 connections on LinkedIn, so I knew if I connected with 100 people per week, in 20 weeks, I'd have more than 10,000 connections. Of course, not everyone will accept your connection request, but this will help you get in the ballpark, and you can refine from there. Building your audience will ensure that the book marketing efforts you put in won't go to waste. It's also good for your business, so this one isn't just about your book.

Once you have the audience, the best way to build buzz around your book is by promoting your book launch. You can decide what your book launch will look like. From low-key to an elaborate event to anywhere in between, a book launch can be anything you want, but even if you choose something more low-key (e.g., sending out an announcement to your email list and posting about it on social media), you still need to promote the launch date.

Think of this as if you were opening a brick-and-mortar store. It's difficult to plan for a grand opening. You need to be far enough along on the construction, build-out, and design that you can be sure you'll be able to welcome people into your store on that date. So you need to be generous in your choice of a date. Also, this doesn't mean that you can't open your store before the grand opening. If you end up being ahead of schedule on construction, you can always do a soft launch where you invite particular people to come to the store for a preview sale.

You can do something similar with your book launch. All you have to do is choose a date (remember that this is a commitment, so you'll need to be sure your book will be published by your "launch date"). As with the soft launch and preview sale above, it's fine for your book to be published and available for purchase on Amazon before your "official" launch date; in fact, this is the way it should work so that there is stock available on the official release date. You could also call it a "soft launch." Or tout the publication date as a way for those attending your official launch event to get their own copy of your book, which they can bring with them to the event later.

Once you've chosen the date for your official launch, decide what you want the launch event to be and how much you want to spend. Could you do a book reading and simple celebration on Zoom? Could you do a reading at your local library or bookstore? Could you rent a local venue like a coworking space, serve snacks, ask a friend to interview you, and give away some copies of the book? Does it make sense to do a fundraiser or encourage guests to make a charitable donation in relation to your book's topic? Get creative and make it your own.

Again, this is a place where you could decide to spend some money. You may want to factor in your book launch event when creating your book marketing budget. If you have a PR team, this is something they may be able to help you plan. If you have friends who pull off fabulous events for their businesses, ask them for advice. They may also be game to help you plan and execute your launch party.

Whatever you decide, plan it far in advance and ask your biggest supporters to save the date. Think of it as a project you are managing. Writing a book is a huge accomplishment, and you don't want to let it pass by without celebrating your win.

YOUR BOOK LAUNCH TEAM

Every author fantasizes about other people helping to market their book for *free*, and for good reason. Word of mouth is still the number one driver of all book sales, whether self-published or traditionally published. As we near the end of the book writing process, my ghostwriting clients have a lot of questions about marketing and promoting. They say, "I can't handle all of the marketing by myself; how do I recruit the help of others?" The best way to kick-start word of mouth is to create a book launch team.

Notice that, while there could be some overlap, your book launch team is not the same thing as your beta readers. While beta readers read a clean draft of your manuscript and give you feedback that you'll use to make your final version even better, your book launch team will get an advance copy of the final version to read so that they can leave glowing reviews and talk about your book with their audiences. Their job is not to give you feedback on the content of your book but to promote your book.

You can enlist people to join your marketing efforts by letting them read your book early. For many readers, it's a cool perk to be among the first ones in the know. These early adopters get to be ahead of the curve. More important for you, they get to tell their friends, "I'm reading a great book that isn't yet available to the public." Never underestimate the promotional power of your biggest supporters.

Those who agree to be on your book launch team are your biggest supporters.

But how do you find these wonderful people and assemble them into an active group that is willing to share the marketing load? This takes some skill. In addition, what should you ask them to do on your behalf?

Follow these six steps:

1. RECRUIT PEOPLE FROM YOUR AUTHOR EMAIL LIST AND SOCIAL MEDIA PAGES.

Start the recruiting process with those who already have an affinity for you and your book. Reach out to individuals on your email list and those following you on social media. The best people to target are those who engage with your posts and enthusiastically say "yes" when you put out anything new. Also, ask your friends, coworkers, family members, etc.

Send out two to three emails or social media posts that say, "I'd love your help ... " or "Join my launch team and read my new book before anyone else." Don't twist people's arms or use guilt tactics. Consider asking those you know who could most benefit from reading your book and then let people volunteer willingly. Accept everyone who wants to join. If you can get 50–100 recruits, you're in decent shape. But I've worked with authors who have attracted 500–1,000 people. The more ... the merrier.

2. BEGIN RECRUITING FOUR TO SIX WEEKS IN ADVANCE.

Timing is important. I recommend building a launch team four to six weeks before the book publication date. You need to be sure you'll have a full draft ready by the time you're ready to start assembling your team. However, if you ask too far in advance, people will forget, lose interest, and fail to participate. It's also rude to wait until the last minute and beg people for assistance. Give people the courtesy of planning ahead for the time they'll need to commit to reading your book and completing their designated marketing tasks.

To ensure that you're recruiting your team at the right time, make this part of your minimum viable marketing plan (MVMP).

3. COMMUNICATE WITH YOUR TEAM VIA EMAIL.

Some authors use a private group, like a Facebook group, to communicate with their launch teams. However, some authors and launch team members say that approach can be too confusing and unwieldy. Who wants to join another Facebook group anyway? Instead, I recommend putting your launch team on a special email list. Then use email to keep in touch with everyone throughout your book campaign. You should email the team at least once a week with updates to let them know how things are progressing, share any good news you receive, and keep them in the loop about upcoming launch ideas and any special events.

4. SEND YOUR LAUNCH TEAM AN ADVANCE READER COPY.

Once you've recruited your team, send everyone a copy of your book to read in advance (aka Advance Reader Copy, or ARC). If you self-publish, consider an inexpensive service such as BookFunnel.com to send digital ARCs to your team and monitor participation.

I was part of a launch team, and the author used BookFunnel. It was a really easy process from my end. I just clicked to download the PDF, and I could read it. So I definitely recommend this resource.

If your book is traditionally published, get permission from your publisher to send a full copy of your manuscript ahead of time to your launch team. Some publishers will provide a link to read your ARC on a protected website to prevent piracy. Or they may send a PDF file with a watermark embedded for protection.

The key is to get ARCs to your team at least two to three weeks before your launch date. That way, they have time to get familiar enough with your book to write a review and maintain enthusiasm. If you send ARCs too far in advance, people can forget about it and lose momentum before your campaign starts.

5. DEFINE THE REQUESTED MARKETING ACTIVITIES UP FRONT.

As you recruit people to your book launch team, clearly state the marketing activities you expect everyone to complete. Tell people there is work involved as part of your team. Set the expectations up front. I recommend asking everyone to complete the following marketing activities (listed in order of importance):

- Post a review of your book on Amazon and other online retailers.
- Preorder your book or buy a copy for a friend.
- Share posts (you should write them yourself to make it easier for them to share) about your book on their social media, blogs, and e-newsletters.
- Tell their friends about your preorder bonuses (if you're offering any, e.g., some authors offer a special bonus chapter to readers who preorder) and encourage early sales.

As a rule of thumb, don't expect everyone on your launch team to participate. In many cases, only 30–50% may take action. That's a typical response, which is why you should recruit as many people as possible. If the majority of your team completes the activities listed above, you'll get incredible word of mouth for free.

Preorders are especially important from a book marketing perspective. This means you will get early reviews that can help boost sales. It also signals to the publisher that your book is on track to do really well.

6. REWARD YOUR TEAM FOR HELPING YOU.

I don't believe in bribing people to join your book launch team. But I do believe in thanking and rewarding people for helping to promote your book. Besides giving everyone an advance copy of your book, you can show appreciation in several ways, such as:

- Conducting a private teleconference or video webinar and taking Q&A
- Sending a personal email or handwritten note thanking people for their support
- Creating free bonus content and distributing it to your team
- Letting your team know about any special sales or discounts before anyone else
- Offering a one-on-one session of some sort with book launch team members

Book launch teams are a crucial part of the author experience. Because distribution is key, you need people to get the word out. There's nothing like watching dozens, if not hundreds, of people spread word of mouth on your behalf.

Before you release your book, use these six steps to build an effective book launch team. Then, sit back and watch as they create a growing wave of marketing momentum that can jump-start your book sales.

Chapter 15

HOW TO USE A BOOK TO MARKET YOUR BUSINESS

Yay! You've made it to the final chapter of this book. That means you're almost ready to make a go of this thing. How are you feeling? If you're experiencing a lump in your throat, you're not alone. I haven't been able to fully swallow since I started writing this book. It's terrifying to put your big, hairy, audacious ideas into the world. If it were easy to write and publish a business book, then every business owner would have a book. The thing to remember is that the book is not an end in itself. It's a means of marketing your business. It's a key element of your thought leadership ecosystem, and it can provide you with a lot of clarity around your messaging.

Thinking of your book as a means to market your business might actually make it easier to write. This means that your book doesn't have to be earth-shatteringly spectacular. It doesn't have to be perfect or even "the best" in its category. It simply has to provide your audience with the transformation they need. And because this is a business book, you already know that what you're sharing has transformed others. The proof of concept is in the work you do with your clients every day. I hope this gives you a lot of confidence as you write.

Also, if you have been waiting to start writing your book until you finish reading this, I want you to stop right now and start writing. Go back to the pre-reading exercises in the introduction once again and consider doing some mind mapping. Start with the smallest possible step and take action. Then you can come back and finish reading this chapter.

The question to answer in this chapter is how best to use your book to market your business. Because you aren't living under any delusions that your book will be breaking any book sales records, you can relax about book sales and instead focus on the other revenue that comes as a result of your having written this book. As I say in the previous chapter, distribution is important, and you're leaving money on the table if you don't properly market your book, but you're not leaving money on the table because of the lost book sales. You're leaving money on the table because of the loss of the people who would have bought your book and realized *they need to work with you*. This shift in perspective should also take some of the pressure off. You are measuring success with your book in a different way from bestselling authors, not in terms of book sales but in terms of visibility, awareness, and leads generated for your business.

Circling back to the business case for your book, success, for you, could look like:

- Prospects finding you and saying "yes" to working with you because of your book
- Confidence gained around your own thought leadership
- Increasing demand that allows you to increase your prices

- New ideas for products and services or other revenue streams for your business
- New content ideas to fold into your thought leadership ecosystem
- Speaking opportunities popping up and your book being the factor that tips you into winning those opportunities
- Podcast hosts wanting to have you on their shows to talk about your book

In addition to setting goals about the transformation you want your readers to take and marketing your book, I also want you to set goals for what you want your book to do for your business. I hope that the picture of how your book would help you grow your business was clear in your mind from the beginning. But if you need to clarify that picture, now is the time to think and write up your plan.

YOUR BOOK, THE BEST MARKETING TOOL FOR YOUR BUSINESS

I started writing this book because a friend convinced me that writing books for others is my superpower. (I shouldn't have needed convincing. I know this to be true. Still, it was helpful to be reminded.) I had something different in mind. In fact, I've started writing two other books in the past few years. But I'm so grateful that she didn't simply go along with what I was saying about needing more time to nail down my big idea, because this book makes so much sense in terms of how it helps me market my business. If you need a friend to remind you of your superpower, don't be afraid to reach out and get some reassurance. When you're confident in what you're writing, and you know that you're writing this book to use as a marketing tool, you will be unstoppable.

Let's talk about all the ways you can use your book to market your business:

1. CONSIDER YOUR BOOK AS A CREDIBILITY BOOSTER.

Imagine someone is choosing between whether to work with you or with one of your competitors. Then they discover that you have written a book, and your competitor hasn't. This would be an incentive to at least hop on a discovery call with you. If your prospect is serious about finding someone who does what you do to help them out, they'll do their homework. They'll likely buy your book and start reading. If they like what they see, your book has done a lot of the sales work for you. It's always better to have a discovery call with a warm lead.

We talk about sales success in terms of establishing that know, like, and trust factor. Trust is perhaps the most important piece of this trifecta. Anything you can do to establish trust with prospects gets you further down the road to that sale, and a book is a great way to establish trust. This is especially true if you share the same process you share with your clients in the book, and you give readers a real taste of what it's like to work with you. Obviously, the one-on-one experience will not be the same; it will be better, but even getting a small taste could whet their appetite. If I read a book and it transforms me, you can bet I'm interested in signing up for a one-on-one experience, assuming it's in my budget. Give people a real taste of what it's like to work with you, and it won't be long before you start to hear from prospects who have read your book and make a point of telling you that's why they reached out to you.

Also, if you aspire to be paid to speak, then having a book is a must. A lot of conference organizers will only choose keynote speakers who have written a book. Having a book is basically a credential for getting on certain stages. This is why a lot of coaching organizations encourage their coaches to write books or chapters for anthologies. It establishes credibility for the big stage. Plus, speaking gigs are great places to market and sell your book.

Personally, I don't see becoming a speaker as a separate revenue stream for me (though I'm happy to accept any paid keynote opportunities that come my way). I love speaking to small groups, doing trainings and content strategy workshops. Still, this book will help me grab the attention of organizers who have entrepreneur communities or who host "lunch and learns." It will open doors to borrowing audiences and getting in front of my target audience. So even if you don't have dreams of being on the big stage, a book can help you find other speaking opportunities that can be just as good for your business.

2. GIVE YOUR BOOK AWAY TO CLIENTS AND PARTNERS.

In the introduction, I made the distinction between two extremes: people who say writing a business book is valuable only if you become a bestselling author and those who say you should forget about selling your book at all. Throughout this book, I've been making the case for a middle way. Sure, you want to sell books, but while book sales are not your only goal, distribution is important. You can strategically give books away, then. But I don't want you giving your book away like a business card. Many authors use their book as a free gift, a bonus, or an incentive to work with them. I've heard many describe their book as a $10 business card. Why give away a simple business card when you can give away a whole book? This is not a bad strategy, but keep in mind that it can also seem a bit desperate. It's all in the delivery.

I have certainly received copies of books over the years that I didn't really want or ask for and immediately donated because I wasn't interested in reading the book, and the author who gave it to me didn't even take the time to discover whether I was their target reader. This automatically undercuts your book's value. The lesson here: Don't give away copies of your book willy-nilly. Take the time to get to know whether someone would benefit from reading your book before offering it as a free gift. Ask them if they'd like a copy. Don't simply assume everyone wants free books, and don't be afraid to sell it if you know it would provide value.

Another good way to use your book as an incentive is to bundle it with a set of products, services, or a course. If you have created an online course, writing a book as a supplement to the course is a great way to add value to the course and renew interest in both. You can consider this angle as you write your book too. Perhaps your book could serve as a workbook for your course. It might also be a good stand-in for those who aren't ready for the full course.

Consider how your book fits into the wider set of offerings you deliver or want to deliver in the near future. There might be prospects who aren't ready for your full program but who need an easy entrance point into your world. There may be prospects who can't afford your products or services, and your book could allow you to capture this revenue stream. There are a number of different options here.

3. YOUR BOOK COULD LEAD TO INCREASED DEMAND.

If you do a good job of marketing your book, then you should see a bump in demand for your work. It's possible that any money you invest in getting your book written (which includes the time you spend writing your book, of course) will be the best marketing dollars you spend. Not only does your book give you virtually endless content to repurpose, but it also gives podcast hosts and event organizers an additional reason to pay attention to your pitch. At a minimum, your book should lead to increased exposure and PR opportunities, which should boost demand for your services. And this would be on top of the increased demand coming from those getting exposed to you and your work as a result of finding your book.

The book is where true thought leadership happens. While your social media presence, blog articles, Substack, and other industry articles are pieces of your thought leadership ecosystem, your book is the culmination of all those various thoughts. The smaller stuff likely only scratches the surface for you. A book gives you the opportunity to dive deep and take your ideal clients with you. It's smart to pay attention to who is picking up your book. It might give you some new ideas about your ideal client, especially if you start to hear from groups of people who are reading your book together for a book club, say.

So it should be clear by this point that although you likely won't get rich selling copies of your book, your book can be a springboard for business. It all goes back to figuring out what the business case is for your book. If you can see how your book will help you grow your business, then you need a book. And if you need a book, then you should write that book as quickly as possible so you can get back to other revenue-generating activities. Stop overthinking your book and underthinking everything else.

If, however, you don't have a business case for your book, then now is not the time to write a book. There's no shame in that. There may come a time when it's easier for you to see how a business book would boost your business, and there's nothing wrong with letting your idea bake a bit longer. It might seem strange for me to talk you out of writing your book, but if I can save you from having an unsatisfying experience, and the decision not to write your book helps you to grow your business, then I've done my job. Writing a business book is not an end in itself. Writing a business book that will help you grow your business is what we're here for.

Finally, I want to remind you that you are an expert without ever having written a single word. Your idea chose to manifest itself through you *because* you are the expert. Your book is not a credential. It's not a badge. It needs to pull its weight, or it doesn't belong. And it's worth remembering that there are thousands of ways you can cultivate your thought leadership ecosystem without writing a book. Think through this decision carefully, and if it's go time, then go!

CONCLUSION

As you read this final section, you might have a sinking feeling. It may be dawning on you that after you finish the next few pages, you won't have any more excuses not to get to work. Eek! You're on deck. If you're not exactly cheering, "Put me in, Coach" by this point, that's okay. Take a deep breath. I'm serious. Take a deep breath. Then keep reading.

Go back to your pre-reading exercises. Look at your checklist. You know you should write this book.

Look at your book idea. It's beautiful. It's ready to come into the world. The idea is yours because it chose you as the steward to bring it into the world.

Look at your book's why. This is how you will connect with your reader. Not only is your idea ready to come into the world, but your readers are also ready to receive this idea. Now is the time.

Finally, look at your list of obstacles. Which one is looming largest in your mind right now? What is the smallest step you can take to overcome or push past that obstacle this week? Maybe it's writing one sentence. Maybe it's writing for ten minutes. Maybe it's outlining your book or your first chapter. Maybe it's identifying someone to head up your support system. Maybe it's creating your marketing plan. Whatever it is, taking action is the best way to move out of overwhelm. So take action.

Next, revisit Part 1 and come up with a plan for writing your book. Remember to create some guardrails for yourself here. You might find that planning feels ever so comfortable, cozy even. You can get stuck here for months, and I don't love that for you. Give yourself a time limit—a day or two is best. Come up with a mind map and a rough outline. Do some simple math and set your word count goal. Then start writing.

Easy for me to say. Sure, it's all much easier said than done. But I've also done it for my clients and now for myself, so I know that it can be done. As I've written this book, I've tried to stick to my own advice as much as possible, and there's nothing magical about me. I faced many of the same challenges as you will face in writing this book. I also faced many of these challenges when writing books for my ghostwriting clients. And there's no magic fix (unless you want to hire a ghostwriter to write your book for you). What I recommend here is the closest thing I have found to a magic fix. I've revealed all my secrets for making writing a book seem like a superpower. The biggest secret is figuring out the fastest way to get to a complete, messy, first draft.

It doesn't matter if you don't feel ready to write, or you don't feel like you have enough ideas. The ideas will come if you let them. The door is through your fingers. Start wherever you hear that voice in your head. Trust that voice. When that inner critic starts chirping, shut that sh*t down. Tell your critic there will be time to voice their concerns during the editing stage, and get back to writing your messy draft. You will feel better when you have that draft done. For now, the only thing you should be thinking about is hitting your word count goal. Your idea is counting on you. This is how you take care of your idea. Let everything else take care of itself.

Right now, your book is unwritten. But it won't be for long. There's a good reason your idea chose you—you're the expert. Still, you have a business to run. You can't let that needy little idea supersede every other revenue-generating task. Like every piece of marketing content you create, your book has a bigger purpose beyond being an outlet for your musings. It has to fit into your brand's broader ecosystem. Please don't lose track of that bigger purpose. Every suggestion I've shared in this book drives you toward staying focused on the big picture.

HOW ARE YOU FEELING ABOUT THOSE THREE BIG TRAPS WE IDENTIFIED?

Trap #1: Doing too much planning.

Trap #2: Overthinking the writing.

Trap #3: Underthinking the positioning, publishing, and promoting.

Earlier I said that writing your book while running your business could be one of the hardest things you'll ever do. I also said I hope it's one of the most satisfying things you'll ever do, because if writing your book yourself is all pain and no satisfaction, then you shouldn't do it. I stand by this proclamation. It might be tough to see how satisfaction has anything to do with it when you're standing in the batter's circle taking your practice swings and contemplating taking the plate against the world-famous, premier pitcher in the league. That's probably how you're feeling now, and you have two choices: knock it out of the park or strike out. And that's exactly why I want you to shift into action.

The satisfaction comes from smashing those word count goals out of the park. It comes from seeing your idea take shape and thinking about the possibilities. Stay focused on this abundance and you'll start to feel the momentum. It's addictive. Striking out isn't even an option here.

As I write these words, I'm finishing up a two-day writing retreat at the beach with my dear friend Jill, the one who nudged me to write this book. I've written nearly 10,000 words over the course of two days. How did I do it? I set up eight 90-minute writing blocks and hit my goal of writing 1,250 words each block. This is one way to write your book. You can do the same, or you can do something else that works for you. I recommend writing in 90-minute sprints because it works well for me, but if you have trouble concentrating for that long, perhaps 30-minute blocks work better for you. Whatever helps you get words on the page is fine.

This brings me to one more important trap that writers fall into:

Trap #4: Quitting before you feel the satisfaction.

If it feels too hard and like too much of a grind, then you haven't made it far enough. There's a tightrope that I'm trying to walk here. On the one hand, if you don't feel the satisfaction of writing a book, you shouldn't write the book. On the other hand, it's easy to quit before you feel the satisfaction. It's a tricky thing to navigate. My best advice for determining whether you've come far enough is to keep going. If you have momentum, if you're able to continue to meet your word count goals each week or even write *something* each week, then it's not time to quit. If you struggle to write every week—not because you're swamped and barely have time to eat but because you do everything you can think of to avoid writing—then you're not likely to feel the satisfaction of writing, and you should find a different way to cultivate your thought leadership ecosystem or find an alternative way to bring that idea into the world.

Not every business owner should write a book. It's possible that your book should remain unwritten—at least for now. As with so many aspects of running a business, there are many ways to build a thought leadership ecosystem. Writing a book only makes sense for you if you have a business case for your book.

I know that at different points in this book, I tow the line between validating your pessimism and painting a rosy picture that seems too good to be true. This largely follows my own thinking about my book and my business, I'm afraid. It's the only way I know. I'm trying to be real, so it's a reflection of how I have been thinking about this project. This book is a snapshot of my brain, and I hope that it motivates you to take a snapshot of yours. Writing your business book will be the hardest and most satisfying thing you ever do for your business. It could also be the best thing you do for your business. There will be hard parts, but when you push through, you will find a new gear you didn't even know you had, and this will benefit you in ways you can't even begin to imagine. I'll let you know when I start to experience those benefits (I've already started to experience a few). They're coming down the pike.

I started this book by suggesting that it was written by a business owner for business owners. I want you to write your book from this perspective. You don't have to morph into becoming a writer to get your business book done. In fact, the result will be better if you stand in your power as a business owner. You're the big idea expert. That's why your idea chose you to bring it into the world. If you stay grounded in this symbiotic relationship, the sky's really the limit.

Ready. Set. Go. Write well!

ACKNOWLEDGMENTS

Before I get to thanking all the people who have made this book possible, I want to share this caveat: acknowledgments sections are a field of land mines. When I wrote the acknowledgments section for my dissertation, I heard from so many people who were upset about not being named individually, not being included at all, not being correctly mentioned, and not being sufficiently effusively thanked. And that was just a dissertation, which was technically published, I suppose—it does exist in the library at Washington University in St. Louis, I think—and which I hope doesn't receive anywhere near the number of readers as this book.

I don't remember, but in my defense, I probably wrote my acknowledgements in 15 minutes or less on the very day I had to turn in the final version. I treated it as a throwaway, and I regret that slightly.

I realize that's not a really good defense, but I was tired and inexperienced, and I really didn't see much of a reason to share credit for my accomplishment. That oversight was the result of a mind steeped in the hard-nosed, scarcity mindset that one lives and breathes while existing in the shadow of the ivory tower. Again, it's not a really good defense, but gratitude isn't compatible with scarcity. I'm in a much more abundant state of mind now. This time around, I want to do justice to this section because I do owe a debt of gratitude to the many supportive people in my life. Still, I'm sure I will f*ck it up, but here I go, walking through the minefield anyway. Wish me luck!

Thanks are due to Jill Delston, who wouldn't let me weasel out of writing this book (no matter how hard I tried). When I first started, I joined Brainstorm Road, which is a really beautiful community of people practicing, shipping, and sharing something every week for six months. Brainstorm Road deserves its own credit in helping me get this book written. I'm especially grateful to those who stopped by my Scratchpad to lend words of encouragement and kind yet pointed feedback, and who cheered me on for six months. But back to Jill. When I first started, I thought I'd spend six months in Brainstorm Road brainstorming my book topic idea. When I told Jill, she immediately picked up the phone and said, "What are you even talking about? You're going to write a book about how to write a business book." I had what I thought was a grander vision. I didn't want to write another how-to book about writing, but she quickly convinced me that I wasn't just writing another how-to book about writing. I spent the next two months pounding out the first draft and the next seventeen months creating the book you hold in your hands (as well as publishing, positioning, and promoting). I'm also grateful to Jill for spending a few days at the beach with me on a glorious writing retreat, which was instrumental in getting me to a complete, messy first draft within two months of starting.

I also want to thank the regular participants of my weekly cowriting sessions, Jill, Jen, Evangeline, Ravit, and Emily. "Write the Thing!" is something I started during the pandemic. We meet most Fridays for

90 minutes on Zoom, usually to rant and rave a bit before getting down to writing. It's free and open to anyone, so if you'd like to join us, let me know. It's part support group, part accountability, and always productive. I wrote and edited a good chunk of this book during those WTT sessions.

Thanks to Heidi Scott Giusto for being a beta reader and for giving me invaluable feedback on an early draft. Thanks also for volunteering to write a blurb and be on my book launch team. Our quarterly business retreats never fail to leave me feeling challenged (in a good way!) and extra motivated.

Thanks to Podge Thomas, who helped me operationalize not only planning and writing this book (and my whole damn business) but also figuring out my budget for publishing and promoting. The Pocket PhD would not be what it is without you.

Thanks to Jessica Lackey, who was also writing a book at the same time and agreed to meet with me to brainstorm about our books once per month.

Thanks to my LinkedIn community, who assured me that there were real live people out in the world who wanted to read my musings about writing a business book.

Thanks to my papa and mom, who infused me with a fierce independence even when it was probably not very convenient for them. Thanks to Joel, Laura, Ben, and Elizabeth for making being the oldest something I proudly wear as a badge of honor. Thanks to Liam, Henry, Odin, and Oliver for being the best nephews. I'll always be up for a playdate.

Thanks to all the people I've known throughout my academic career teaching philosophy. Over the years, you all molded me into a better thinker, a better writer, and the sweetest little bad*ss anyone has ever met. I wouldn't be where I am today without those earlier experiences (for better or worse).

Finally, I want to thank my husband, without whose endless love, support, and restaurant-quality breakfasts this book wouldn't have been possible. He inspires me every day with his own big ideas, letter-writing, quirky expressions, and acronyms I can never guess and is the absolute best at brainstorming title ideas. I love you more, J!

ABOUT THE AUTHOR

Emily Crookston is the ghostwriter for rebels, renegades, and mavericks. She helps thought leaders turn their big ideas into business books. As the Owner and Decider of All Things at The Pocket PhD, she and her team help entrepreneurs and experts cultivate their Thought Leadership Ecosystem, a system of interdependent content pieces (short- and long-form) connected by a dynamic strategy that takes into account distribution, audience, and business goals.

If you ask, Emily will tell you that her favorite thing about being a ghostwriter is discovering quirky, cool ways to translate complex ideas for nonexpert audiences. Her work has appeared in *Forbes*, *Entrepreneur*, *Ellevate*, *Psychology Today*, *Rolling Stone*, *Inman*, *SmartBrief*, and *ThriveGlobal*.

Emily is also a former philosophy professor, a speaker, and a podcast guest. When she's not writing intensely, she's most likely practicing yoga intensely. She lives for coffee shops that play great music to write to and desserts topped with *real* whipped cream.